ALSO BY JAMES CARVILLE

Take It Back (coauthored with Paul Begala)

Had Enough? (with Jeff Nussbaum)

Stickin'

Buck Up, Suck Up . . . and Come Back When You Foul Up
(coauthored with Paul Begala)

. . . And the Horse He Rode In On

We're Right, They're Wrong

All's Fair (coauthored with Mary Matalin)

40 MORE YEARS

How the Democrats Will
Rule the Next Generation

James Carville

with Rebecca Buckwalter-Poza

Simon & Schuster

NEW YORK LONDON TORONTO SYDNEY

To the people who live on the disappearing
coastline of South Louisiana

Simon & Schuster
1230 Avenue of the Americas
New York, NY 10020

First Simon & Schuster hardcover edition May 2009

SIMON & SCHUSTER and colophon are registered trademarks
of Simon & Schuster, Inc.

For information about special discounts for bulk purchases,
please contact Simon & Schuster Special Sales at
1-800-456-6798 or business@simonandschuster.com.

The Simon & Schuster Speakers Bureau can bring authors to your live event. For
more information or to book an event contact the Simon & Schuster Speakers
Bureau at 1-866-248-3049 or visit our website at www.simonspeakers.com.

Designed by Paul Dippolito

Manufactured in the United States of America

3   5   7   9   10   8   6   4   2

Library of Congress Cataloging-in-Publication Data

Carville, James.
40 more years : how the Democrats will rule the next generation / James Carville.
        p.   cm.
Includes bibliographical references.
1. Democratic Party (U.S.)   2. Politics, Practical—United States.
3. United States—Politics and government—21st century.
I. Title.   II. Title: Forty more years.
JK2316.c32   2009
324.2736—dc22   2009000477
ISBN-13: 978-1-4165-6989-3
ISBN-10:   1-4165-6989-8

Contents

Preface

Every four years, Americans hold a presidential election. Somebody wins, and somebody loses. That's life. But 2008 was an anomaly. The election of Senator Barack Obama is part of something far bigger than four or even eight years in the White House. Since 2004, Americans have been witnessing—and participating in—the emergence of a Democratic majority that will last not four but forty years.

American presidential politics is generally not a back-and-forth enterprise. There are eras in which one party dominates. Today, a Democratic majority is emerging, and it's my hypothesis, one I share with a great many others, that this majority will guarantee the Democrats remain in power for the next forty years.

That sounds like a radical proposition. In reality, it is a proposition borne out by history. Stock pickers look at stock trends. Bettors check the horses. Here we're going to look at the history books. Time for some basic civics. Look at the years from 1896 to 1932, then 1932 to 1968, Eisenhower,* then 1968 to 2008. (Okay, that includes Clinton and half a Carter term.) So now we're at 2008, and we're two years into a congressional sea change and just embarking on the first term of an Obama-Biden administration.

The waning Republican majority grew out of a reaction to the 1960s, and race played a big part of it. (I don't want to hear otherwise, it did—take it from a boy who grew up in Louisiana.) Go back and read Kevin Phillips's *The Emerging Republican Majority* if you need to do so.

---

* Barely a Republican; a Clinton democrat.

Now the reaction to the 1960s is in its last throes. The Republican majority has always been based upon whites and, in particular, white males. They have to shift. The bulwark of Republican electoral strength is disappearing. Republicans are now a regional party heavily dependent upon disappearing demographics. Nearly half of all Republican-held seats in Congress are in the South. Not to open old wounds, Zell Miller had the right title and the wrong party: A National Party No More.

Republicans feel the importance of the white male vote slipping away. Just listen to Pat Buchanan. They're absolutely offended at the attack on the white male and his decline in society. They've got a point. I've been a white man for some years and can't tell you what it's like just walking down the street. Not to be shrill about it, but I'm sick of never seeing white men in any positions of power.

The Democratic majority started to emerge in 2004. That was the thirty-six-year point. Now it's 2008, and it's time for the beginning of a forty-year period of Democratic dominance. The definitive victory of President Obama this year—which included Indiana, North Carolina, Nevada, New Mexico, and a variety of previously "purple" states—and the sheer tide of electoral votes and congressional seats Democrats won this year should silence even the most reality-averse of critics. From the sheer incompetence of the Bush administration to the poisoning of the Republican Party brand among Americans to the demographic disadvantage conservatives face, all signs suggest that 2008 will be the first of many victories for the Democrats. This isn't to say Democrats will win every election for the next forty years. In eras of party dominance, parties will still lose elections, both congressional and a periodic presidential.

I keep a running list of the moments that toppled the Republican majority. It's quite possible the point at which this age ended was when the Chief Justice of the Supreme Court seemed on the verge of tears when he had to make Exxon pay. Another contender, an event that happened that spring, was the day that Bush's liaison to religious groups resigned from the administration for multiple acts of egregious plagiarism. I'd also nominate the February 2008 date when the public found out that ExxonMobil was earning record profits while Americans were paying record-high gas prices. As consumers were paying $4 a gallon last year, putting off vacations, and changing their spending habits to adjust to rising gas prices, Exxon made $12 billion in a single quarter, more than any company in U.S. history—until that point. In December 2008, Exxon reported third-quarter profits of nearly $15 billion, dwarfing their previous two record-setting quarters.[1]

Not even John McCain could save the GOP. The Republicans nominated John McCain despite themselves. Let's give John McCain his due. McCain really is a patriot. Watch the footage of him from the POW camp in Hanoi. I cried. McCain had a chance to leave the prison camp early, and he refused to do it. McCain is a man of remarkable courage, and I have no reason to think he's not deeply patriotic. (Sarah Palin is another story.)

Of the contenders for the Republican nomination, McCain may have been the furthest from being a Bush Republican per se, if not the maverick he claimed. But McCain's campaign was doomed from the start. The obvious is sometimes the real answer. Someone asked Ray Charles, "What's the worst part about being blind?" He somewhat famously responded, "Not being able to see."

In 2008, candidates for the Republican presidential nomination faced two truisms. The first was that no one could get the Republican nomination by being anti-Bush. The second was that no candidate who was close to George W. Bush could win the general election. McCain got caught in between. McCain didn't help matters by his Hail Marys to the far right, the most memorable of which was a previously little-known first-term governor from the state of Alaska.

The question McCain repeatedly failed to answer was this: Does he understand what's going on in the world around him? In a newly diverse, newly Democratic political landscape, McCain was violently out of touch, clinging to a set of policies and ideas that, not unlike the senator, are well past their prime. Republicans never let go of their low-wage, no-regulation economic platform, even floating as a possible secretary of the Treasury Phil Gramm, architect of the deregulation of the banking and lending industry, as the politics Gramm put into place set the stock markets tumbling around Americans' ears.

It's a new world. For example, the economic crisis last summer and the bailout marked the end of unregulated markets. Everyone in the world knows that the little boys and girls in Wall Street here at home and the brokers and traders around the world can't stick to playing in their own sandboxes. They're too greedy. It'd be fine if these racketeers just lost their money, but there are others involved. I'm all for intervening where Wall Street's right to make or lose money begins to infringe on the public's right to survive— and, news flash, so is everyone else.

If the traders and bankers want to go invest in Pets.com, I don't care. If they want to buy IPO Microsoft, that's fine. If it's Pets.com, you lose all your money; if it's Microsoft, you're a gazillionaire. That's not really the public's business. But when you interject yourself in, let's say, the subprime market, you send a bunch of people out to sell to—to put it mildly—a bunch of uninformed people, a product that you know full well they can't pay for in the end. That causes bank failures and a real estate bust, because, remember, when the house is foreclosed on, it affects everyone else's mortgage in the neighborhood.

The Democratic Party in American politics is stronger than ever before. Obama created a new party. He brought new people in all across the country, and in 2008 those new people were donating, registering, and voting alongside the existing base of Democratic voters. I'll take a moment to note here that the revitalization of the Democratic Party has occurred despite, not because of, Howard Dean's disastrous tenure as DNC chair. He was not simply unsuccessful but incompetent, particularly in the case of the 2006 midterm elections. I said then and I'll say again that Dean's leadership was "Rumsfeldian in its incompetence."[2]

Beyond the polling and electoral victories signaling the emergence of a new Democratic majority (and painfully obvious public sentiment), there's the fund-raising. Money doesn't lie. Let's take a trip back to the primaries. In February 2008, McCain was the Republican nominee already, and he'd won every election in a month while Hillary was on the decline and hadn't won a primary in a month. Yet Hillary was able to raise three times as much money as McCain—it was just $11.6 million for McCain[3] to $35.8 million for Hillary.[4]

The best fiscal evidence of the widespread appetite for change is the fact that Obama blew all fund-raising records out of the water. For a historical comparison, Obama had raised $80.2 million by September 2007 while still more than half a year from being the nominee. John Kerry didn't hit $82.6 million until March 2004. By the end of the election, Obama had raised more than $770.4 million.[5]

Something big is happening here. Much of the credit goes to Barack Obama, but there's a second benefactor we Democrats can look to these days. Only one person can be said to be responsible for the sinking of the Republican Party—yes, of course—George Bush.

This is the story of the decline of the Republican Party and the rise of the Democratic majority, Cajun-style.

Ten Reasons Republicans Should Be Worried

Let me back up. Republicans shouldn't be worried. They should be in agony. They should be throwing up. Republicans better get a better policy on prescription drugs and quickly: they're going to need a lot more Prozac.

The Republican brand is the worst political party brand in history. They're just pathetic at this point. The demographic foundations of the Republican Party are crumbling, and they're being held accountable, very rightly so, for having started a massively expensive and disastrous war and creating an economic catastrophe.

xiiPREFACE

1. Young voters.

2. White men.

3. Unmarried voters.

4. Latinos.

5. Party identification and the Republican brand.

6. Iraq, Afghanistan, Pakistan, etc. In short, the world.

7. Incontrovertible proof of massive incompetence.

8. Flagrant and pervasive corruption.

9. They've been figured out. They've been caught. That's what the 2008 election was about, from the House and Senate to the White House.

10. Republicans deserved the spanking they got, and they know they deserved it. (Of course, there are plenty of perverts in their ranks who might just enjoy it.)

Introduction

When historians or scientists look back over huge cataclysmic events, they generally find some harbinger that went unnoticed at the time.

There's always a warning. If you're a chaos theorist, it's the flapping of the proverbial butterfly's wings in New York that caused a tsunami in Hong Kong. A meteorologist might think of it in terms of a category five hurricane that began as a low-pressure area off the Cape Verde Islands on the African coast. Historians remember the assassination of the Archduke Ferdinand as the spark for World War I.

When future historians begin to examine the absolutely disastrous events during the term of President Bush, from massive incompetence to blatant falsehoods and the trampling of the Constitution to the savaging of the good name of the United States around the world, they will look for one of these events.

The stealing of the election of 2000 in Florida is going to be a leading qualifier. But it isn't the one to focus on, for several reasons. (After all, there's really nothing that unusual in people resorting to the courts to try to win an election that they didn't win in the first place.)

Two events occurred within a sixty-day time frame that really set the stage for the current state of America and, more to the point, the sorry state of the Republican Party. The first was a memo written by Matthew Dowd in late November or early December of 2000. At the time, it probably escaped the majority of Republicans' notice, and it was certainly well under the Democratic and national radar.

1

The exact content and evidence he used is largely unknown. I certainly don't know what exactly was in it, and I don't know of anyone who'd let me borrow a copy as I was writing this book. The best authority on the content of the Matthew Dowd memo that I know of is Thomas Edsall, who wrote about it in *Building Red America*. Here's Edsall's summary of the momentous memo that sealed the fate of the Republicans in 2008 and beyond:

> Dowd analyzed poll data and found that the percentage of voters who could be classified as genuinely "swing" or persuadable voters had shrunk from roughly 24 percent of the electorate, to 6 percent or less. This meant that developing governing and election strategies geared at building up turnout among base votes became much more important than developing governing and election strategies designed to appeal to swing, or middle-of-the-road, voters. Persuading a non-voting conservative, a regular listener to Rush Limbaugh, or a hunter determined to protect gun rights to register and get to the polls became much more important and more cost effective than going after the voter who is having trouble making up his mind as to which candidate to vote for. The result was the adoption of policies designed to please the base (tax cuts for the wealthy, restricting abortion, appointing very conservative judges, opposition to stem cell research) that ran counter to Bush's 2000 claim to be a "uniter, not a divider."[1]

Essentially Dowd concluded that trying to win elections by appealing to people in the middle, the vaunted swing vote, was a waste of time. Dowd posited that the real way to win elections was to appeal to and mobilize base voters. In essence Dowd repackaged a strategy many other Republicans, including Reagan, had used before, playing to the base to get elected, and suggested taking it quite a ways further than the GOP had ever dreamed. The Bush team embraced Dowd's memo enthusiastically.

The Bush administration thoroughly and relentlessly implemented the recommendation of the Dowd memo. The result was the rise of the Christian right in U.S. politics and the establishment of a near neo-theocracy, and, of course, a disastrous war, among other things. That memo may well go down in history as one of the most important, influential political documents of the century (if anyone can find it).

Now we come to our second harbinger of disaster. The Bush administration, like a bunch of teenagers with a new car, was eager to take Dowd's strategy for a test drive as they came into office. They wanted to see how far from the middle, how distant from truth, they could go.

And here let's take a quick minute for Carville's story time. I've got a real good one, courtesy of my friend Terry McAuliffe, who's done exhaustive, and, I might add, unchallenged research on the subject of Republican falsehoods. I'll tell you this story because it gives us great insight into just how far they were willing to go and how great the consequences of such a comparatively small lie were.

When the Bush administration was first moving into the White House, doing whatever it is Republicans do to feel at home, some-one decided the staff would claim that the "Clinton people" trashed the White House.[2] Although I'm not prepared to name a suspect at this point in time, I might venture a general guess that the suspect's initials are Karl Rove.

It was a very involved process, putting out this rumor. The Bush people got creative, giving us an early inkling of that loose relation-ship with the truth we'd see so much of later on. They told every-one that these Clinton maniacs had removed all the "W" keys from the keyboards of the computer. (I have a lot of things in my closet, but no keyboard keys.) Then the Bush folks set about shop-ping this rumor to see if the press would bite, if the Democrats would protest, and generally just see how far they could take the strategy.[3]

Ari Fleischer got out and said that the Bush administration staff would be "cataloging" the extensive vandalism that was being rumored of the Clinton staffers. The exact quote? As reported by the *New York Post*, Fleischer said, "What we are doing is cataloging [what] took place." Fleischer volunteered that the White House might itemize the cost of the pranks to taxpayers, but graciously conceded that the cataloging was "very informal—we're going to note it and that's that. Nothing will ever come of it."[4]

The ease with which Republicans were able to feed fiction into the national news cycle told the White House that (a) they could say whatever they wanted and the press would not challenge them; (b) the Democrats were too confused or afraid to mount a vigorous defense; and (c) the public was willing to believe their lies. It wasn't until May that the media finally conceded to debunk the rumor.[5]

Republicans were so successful that their carefully crafted rumor about the Clinton staffers even resurfaced, no doubt by design, this year during the Obama administration transition. In the *Christian Science Monitor,* Jimmy Orr wrote on January 15, 2009, "Remember eight years ago when dozens of computer keyboards in the White House had the W keys removed?"[6]

The Dowd memo and the story about the Clintons trashing the White House were the flapping of the butterfly's wings that caused the tsunami. They were the low-pressure depression of the Cape Verde Islands that caused a category five storm or the assassination of Archduke Ferdinand in Sarajevo. The Republicans had gotten away with stealing the election, and now they knew they could get away with a lot more.

"How did they get away with this?" It's the question I've been asked most frequently during the Bush era. It has many variations. I hear it every time I give a speech, of course, but also at the grocery store and in line at the movie theater. I can't even go into a men's bathroom without getting asked. People want to know, "Why did the American public let this happen?" "Why didn't the press do something?" And, of course, "Where were the Democrats?"

These pained and anguished cries have been sounding across this country for eight years. Now at last I have a good answer:

They didn't get away with it. They've been caught red-handed, and the public has the whole thing figured out.

That's why on November 4, 2008, a majority of Americans, including those in Bush strongholds, elected Barack Obama president of the United States of America. This book is certainly about rapping Republicans for some of the things they "didn't get away with" and drawing attention to a few things they thought they got away with; but it is also, rather more important, about how Democrats and patriotic Americans can build a coalition to restore the United States to being a prosperous, just, and respected nation.

We'll spend some time on an autopsy of the Bush administration and the McCain campaign, reviewing the parade of horribles that is the policy platform of the contemporary Republican Party, before moving on to an examination of the policy ideas that we really do need in the United States. That means talking about the economy, the environment, energy independence, foreign policy, taxes, and health care.

The second part of the book explores the American political landscape and why it is that the Democrats won the 2008 election. The Republicans have been down before, and the Democrats have won Congress before, and we've still managed to lose. This time we strung our policies together into a coherent, appealing narrative. And we did it with the help of the historically diverse, historically Democratic young people who will be the foundation for a lasting Democratic majority.

Along the way, as I always do, I'll tell a few stories, rehash some old turf, and hopefully make a point or two.

Those of you who paid particular attention to the jacket noticed below my name a second name, that of Rebecca Buckwalter-Poza. She is known to me as Becky. There is an interesting story as to how Becky got to be on the jacket of this book. In the summer of 2005, Becky wrote a letter to my office asking for a job. She began as an intern that fall. Over the past four years she has worked with me on any number of projects here in the United States as well as in Africa, Latin America, and Eastern Europe. When I sat down to do this book, I asked for her assistance. It struck me that if I was going to write a book at the age of 64 that focused on the youth vote, it just might be beneficial to ask someone young to give me a hand. It is a special bonus that she is a member of several rather important demographics that I myself cannot claim to represent— she is, clearly, a young woman, and a Latina to boot. Becky did the research and she helped me assemble the entire book. In fact, she became so indispensable that I decided that I would put her name on the jacket with mine. Her input was particularly valuable in matters relating to technology, the Internet, and, of course, all things youth-related. Five campaigns, four continents, and one book later, Becky is now finishing her degree at Harvard.

CHAPTER 1

Why the Republicans Are Going to Get Spanked Over and Over

The Republicans got spanked in 2008, and they're going to keep getting spanked.

The explanation is simple:

- They've destroyed the myth of conservative competence.
- They're corrupt.
- They've lost the culture war.

The myth of Republican competence and fiscal responsibility is shattered. Trust in the GOP is at a historic low. Less than a quarter of the public trusts Republicans more than Democrats to handle the major issues of our time.[1] Thousands of Americans are still homeless or living in trailers in Louisiana and Mississippi because of the towering blunders of the Bush administration during and following Hurricane Katrina. The invasion of Iraq was, as Martin van Creveld, one of the greatest military historians of our time, said, "the most foolish war since Emperor Augustus in 9 BC sent his legions into Germany and lost them."

It used to be that the Democrats were the urban machine stuffing the ballot boxes, and the Republicans were the suburban party with the reform element. That's all history. By any fair assessment, the Republican Party isn't just a little more corrupt than the Democratic Party; it's a lot more corrupt.

The culture war is over because it didn't exist to begin with. It was a Republican invention that worked for two cycles, in 2002 and 2004, and now they've taken it too far. They've ventured into the land of the absurd, into creationism and pretending that the ice caps aren't melting and the oceans aren't heating up degree by degree.

Early on, it looked like McCain might spare Americans another descent into the culture war in 2008, then he picked Sarah Palin as his running mate. Suddenly his waffling over evolution and creationism was small potatoes. That return to the culture wars of 2002 and 2004 was one of his biggest mistakes.

Americans in general, and the younger generations in particular, have rejected the culture war. This youngest generation of voters that turned out in record numbers in 2008 is historically diverse and quite possibly historically Democratic. They're for gay marriage and against the Iraq War, and they think the government should do more for people. Strangely enough, they're also pretty concerned about the environment.

When I ran the title of this chapter by my Republican friends—the most preeminent writers, strategists, and politicians I could find—none of them contradicted me. Republicans are ready to admit that the Republicans are in real trouble. America doesn't want any more of what the Republicans have to offer, and the Republican Party is in full finger-pointing, backstabbing mode.

In campaigns, there are two slogans: stay the course, and time for a change. Change won in 2006, and it won again in 2008. The American people voted for real shifts in strategy and policy, away from the failed Bush policies and old Rove-style politics and toward a new brand of campaigns and politics. The operative word in the previous sentence, dear reader, is "toward." In 2008, Americans didn't just vote against Bush, they voted *for* Obama and *for* Democrats across the country.

Breakdown of the Essential
Republican Covenant

It's Carville story time again. This time let's hear the one about how Republicans made a pact with the American public.

Once upon a time, the Republicans went to voters with a two-part promise. These guys said, "You may not like us, we may be economic royalists, and we may favor corporations and the wealthy too much, but we can offer you two things that the Democrats can't." People were listening.

"Voters," they said, "we're competent. We start meetings on time, and we're efficient." Then they continued, "And, listen, we're culturally compatible. We own guns and trucks. The Democrats are a bunch of effete east coast elites."

For a long time voters bought into that. But over the last eight years the Republicans have destroyed both pillars of their success. They've exposed themselves as not merely incompetent but completely and utterly deranged.

Breakdown of Competence

Iraq is the greatest and perhaps most immediately obvious proof of Republican incompetence. But there's an embarrassment of riches when it comes to proving how badly the Republicans have hurt Americans in the past eight years.

IRAQ

The real point on Iraq is that, depending on how you calculate it, the war is estimated to cost between $1.5 and $3 trillion. That $3 trillion figure, by the way, comes from Professor Joseph Stiglitz of Columbia University, who only won the Nobel Prize in Economic Sciences. Of course, the cost of the war the Republican Party championed becomes all the more unconscionable in light of the economic crisis they engineered. Lack of oversight, rampant tax cuts, burgeoning budget deficits, failure of regulation, and Republicans' anything-goes attitude toward fiscal policy are at the core of our current economic problems.

What is absolutely stunning is that the Republicans, after committing the United States to a $3 trillion war, were unwilling to commit a trillion dollars toward a stimulus package to get out of what Alan Greenspan said would be the most wrenching economic crisis since World War II. It's like the Republicans started a fire, then blocked the roads to keep firefighters from putting out the fire they started.

Americans will be dealing with the consequences of Republicans' rampant irresponsibility for the foreseeable future, and the Republicans are going to have to pay for what they've done. In early 2009 the Republican party faces its ownership of wars in Iraq and Afghanistan, totaling $12 billion a month, and the fallout over what is, without a doubt, a Republican-induced recession.

Barack Obama has been against the war in Iraq from the start— as have I, by the way—and begins from this eminently sensible and responsible position. Americans can trust the Obama administration to follow through on pushing the Iraqi government to invest in reconstruction rather than leaving that to the United States and its allies, and on withdrawing American troops from Iraq.[2]

KATRINA

For most of the flooding in New Orleans, to say it was the result of a natural disaster is one of these convenient Washington lies. It was no such thing. It was a man-made disaster. The city was supposed to be protected by levees built by the federal government to withstand a category three hurricane. The hurricane that hit the city of New Orleans was at most a low two and could have been just a category one. As a result of shoddy construction the levees broke and most of a great American city was lost.

In any court of law any jury would have found the federal government negligent and it would be forced to indemnify the people who suffered as a result of its negligence. But that's another one of these inconvenient topics that shouldn't be brought up in polite company. It's more fashionable to mumble something about corrupt local politicians or the culture of incompetence and corruption in Louisiana or whatever other inane crap that flies because New Orleans is a thousand miles away.

If anyone has any doubt of just how bad President Bush was, all they have to do is watch footage of that incurious dolt receiving the briefing that a major American city was about to be lost and not asking a single question. Then, after he was told what was going to happen happened, he actually flew over New Orleans and didn't land.[3]

It may be more polite to mumble something about Louisiana's lack of self-sufficiency or corruption and how we need to look forward and not back. But the truth is, Katrina was a massive failure of the federal government. There's not a single parliamentary system in this world in which a government that negligent would have survived twenty-four hours without calling an election.

U.S. COAST GUARD

If there were an agency you think Republicans could run, it would be the U.S. Coast Guard. They're all about security, and the Coast Guard is supposed to be our first line of defense. In December 2006, we found out they not only couldn't run the Coast Guard, they might have done a better job sinking its ships than any military opposition has so far.

From 2003 to 2006, a $17 billion shipbuilding contract with LockheedMartin and NorthropGrumman ballooned to $24 billion. Plans to update current patrol boats failed spectacularly. The boats these contractors tried to convert actually ended up in worse shape. As if that weren't enough, the design for a series of new boats proved an utter failure. They didn't even remember to waterproof the radios they installed. Our Coast Guard cutters were running around with a bunch of radios shorting out constantly until someone figured out that these two private contractors hadn't thought to install waterproof radios on boats.

Appropriately enough, this whole plan was called "Deepwater."[4] More like deep, well, you know. The Bush administration managed to decimate the Coast Guard. My favorite quote on the whole debacle was the *New York Times*' editorial: "In Iraq, lax government oversight and incompetence or profiteering by contractors have disabled reconstruction efforts. Now the same disease is undermining our coastal defenses."[5]

What do Iraq and the Coast Guard have in common? I'll give you a hint: Bush.

Corruption and Cronyism

Obviously you'll have Democrats involved on occasion. I'm not denying that Bill Jefferson and Rod Blagojevich had their problems. But corruption is an institution with these Republicans. It's systemic. They're out of control.

Think about the Republicans' major efforts to ding Democrats on corruption. They spent $25.1 million investigating Democrat Mike Espy over Super Bowl tickets, and it ended in his acquittal.[6]

Anyone want to take a guess at how many Reagan administration officials were convicted, indicted, or investigated? I'll tell you, because unless you're a history nut, there's no way you'd ever come up with the number: it's 138.[7]

The Republican Party is a parade of the corrupt, from Duke Cunningham to Governor Jim Gibbons with his briefcase full of cash and poker chips[8] to Senator Ted Stevens,[9] now a convicted felon whose November 2008 "Checkers" speech left all eyes dry. Lest they feel neglected, let's not forget Tom DeLay, charged with money-laundering and conspiracy, or Jack Abramoff, whose deeds are so notorious he no longer needs an explanation to follow his name. (And when you mention Abramoff, it's only polite to acknowledge Representative Bob Ney, whose involvement and subsequent investigation as a result of Abramoff's outing was spectacular.)

Here, courtesy of *The Washington Post*, are some of the highlights of 2007 and 2008 in corruption for the Republican Party:

August 2007: Sen. Larry Craig (R-ID) was arrested during a sex sting in a Minneapolis airport bathroom.*

September 2007: Rep. Jerry Weller (R-IL) announces he won't run for reelection, just days after the *Chicago Tribune* raised questions about the lawmaker's Nicaraguan land deals.

January 2008: Rep. John Doolittle (R-CA) announces he will not run for reelection amid an ongoing federal probe into his and his wife's connections to the Jack Abramoff scandal.

February 2008: Rep. Rick Renzi (R-AZ) is indicted by a federal grand jury on thirty-five counts, mostly related to federal land exchanges. He had already said he would run for reelection this year, and is now awaiting trial.

April 2008: Sen. Pete Domenici (R-NM), who has already announced that he would retire at the end of the year, is admonished by the Senate Ethics Committee for having called the U.S. attorney in New Mexico to ask about the status of a pending corruption investigation.

July 2008: Sen. Ted Stevens (R-AK) is indicted for allegedly making false statements on his financial disclosure reports regarding gifts he got from oil services firm Veco Corp. and its

---

* The sad tale of Larry Craig's bathroom excursion has landed him on this timeline. What makes him corrupt and not merely pathetic is that he tried to get himself out of the situation by flashing his card and saying, "What do you think of that?" "Craig: I did nothing 'inappropriate' in airport bathroom," CNN, August 2, 2007; www.cnn.com/2007/POLITICS/08/28/craig.arrest/, accessed 8/30/07.

CEO. Stevens vows to fight the charges and says he will still run for reelection.[10] Of course, in October 2008, Stevens was convicted on all seven corruption-related counts and in November he was defeated in his run for re-election by Democrat Mark Begich.

FLORIDA

I talked a bit in the Introduction about Florida and what happened in 2000. I don't know how many times I have to say it, but Al Gore won Florida. Period. I'm including this section against the request of my publisher because, well, as I've said on numerous occasions, I'll never get over it.[11] It's small consolation to bask in the vindication of the 3-point victory Obama won last year in Florida.

Here's a number that tells you everything you need to know about what the Republicans got away with in Florida eight years ago: in Palm Beach, Pat Buchanan received 3,704 votes, although he received only 561 in Miami-Dade and 789 in Broward. Also submitted for your consideration: the fact that 29,000 ballots in Palm Beach were discarded as "undervotes"—no chad was punched—or "overvotes"—multiple chads were punched.[12]

You can't tell me 3,700 residents of Palm Beach voted for Pat Buchanan. No one believes that. If you believe it, then I've got a bridge to sell you. The ballots missed in Palm Beach and Duval County probably cost Gore about 113,000 votes.[13] Bush also threw in improperly submitted military ballots and overseas ballots and managed to stop the Miami-Dade recount, which was showing a clear victory for Gore.[14]

A friend named Beth Hellman tells me that her mother-in-law is still recovering from the disillusionment and outrage of 2004. Many of the residents of her Florida community are Holocaust survivors. As important as voting is to them, she says, they'd rather abstain than vote for Pat Buchanan. But if you look at the figures, that's just what the Republicans claim happened in communities all over Florida.

Of course, the Republicans had been hard at work disenfranchising Democrats in Florida for a while. The U.S. Civil Rights Commission concluded that in the lead-up to the 2000 presidential election, charming Florida secretary of state Katherine Harris and her cohort of Republican cronies had improperly scrubbed voting rolls of "felons," 180,000 of whom were legally able to vote. Not to belabor the obvious, but Harris's run on the rolls was obvious, blatant, and offensive disenfranchisement—of those excluded, 54 percent were African-Americans.[15]

In 2008, Republicans got up to the same old tricks—this time with little success. Over summer and fall, the Republican National Committee and the McCain campaign flooded Florida mailboxes with lies about Obama's voting record and his economic plan,[16] attempts to tie Obama to Iranian president Mahmoud Ahmadinejad,[17] and, of course, mailers giving voters incorrect information about voting sites.[18]

While we're in the midst of the history lesson, let's review one more notable fact about the 2000 election: every reputable postelection analysis found that Gore won Florida. The National Opinion Research Center (NORC) at the University of Chicago was hired by a consortium of media outlets to conduct the definitive study on who won the disputed Florida election. Unsurprising, NORC concluded that, "under a full accounting, Gore most likely would be president."[19]

Want more proof? Here's what the *New York Times* reported: "A six-month investigation by The New York Times of this chapter in the closest presidential election in modern American history shows that the Republican effort had a decided impact. Under intense pressure from the Republicans, Florida officials accepted hundreds of overseas absentee ballots that failed to comply with state laws."[20] For more on this, keep reading to the *Res Judicata* chapter.

As the years pass, the evidence keeps piling up. Americans now have overwhelming, incontrovertible proof that Florida was stolen, and it's just one part of the body of evidence that proves Republicans are corrupt.

JUSTICE DEPARTMENT

Two dispositive words for you on the topic of Republican corruption, dear reader: Justice Department. To my great joy, one of the first post-election headlines questioned whether Obama would be investigating Alberto Gonzales and the Justice Department. If you'll recall, Obama voted against Gonzales's nomination, and he called for Gonzales to be replaced in the midst of the Justice Department controversies.[21] That bodes well. Although it is no doubt unnecessary, allow me to formally and clearly express my support for a thorough and unrelenting investigation of Alberto Gonzales and the Bush Justice Department.

Let's review the last few years in the Justice Department. They seem to have had some trouble with understanding the parameters of hiring. Or rather, Attorney General Gonzales demonstrated the same creativity and flexibility when it comes to the truth and the Constitution as the rest of the Bush administration.

There was Monica Goodling. Ms. Goodling graduated from televangelist Pat Robertson's law school at Regent University in 1999. (It's worth noting here that since 2001, the Bush administration has hired no fewer than 150 graduates of Regent University, which graduates only 150 students each year.)[22] Despite her youth and inexperience, or perhaps because of it, given it's the Bush administration we're talking about here, Goodling rose quickly to become senior counselor to Attorney General Gonzales and White House liaison for the Justice Department.

At Gonzales's side, Goodling helped lead the effort to pack the Justice Department with Bush conservatives. Goodling admitted to the House Judiciary Committee that she'd "crossed the line," hiring based on ideological rather than professional or academic credentials.

I'm well acquainted with line-crossing. But, you know, to me, crossing the line is making an off-color joke in mixed company or maybe sticking your foot in your mouth on television. (I do both with some frequency.) Subverting the Justice Department and the U.S. Constitution is less "crossing" the line than trampling it.

Goodling even checked on applicants' political donations during her deliberations.[23] When questioned about the discussion she had with Gonzales about the hiring (and firing) at the Justice Department right before her testimony before the House Judiciary Committee, Goodling just said that he'd made her a bit "uncomfortable."[24]

That's something you'd only hear in the Bush administration.

Goodling's resignation was just the beginning. The more layers you peeled away, the clearer it was how deeply rooted corruption and cronyism were in the DOJ under Bush. Back in 2002, Attorney General John Ashcroft, the guy who lost an election to a dead man in Missouri, changed the hiring process for internships and honors programs so that political appointees would be able to influence the screening process.[25] Now, in 2008, we find that, unsurprising, officials have done their best to pack the DOJ with Bush ideologues.

In June 2008, the Justice Department's Office of Inspector General and Office of Professional Responsibility released a report stating that the department had been throwing out left-leaning applicants for internships and the honors programs. Applicants with connections to Planned Parenthood and the American Constitutional Society got nixed. Top law students from Ivy League schools were kicked to the curb for using "leftist commentary and buzzwords" like "environmental justice" and "social justice."[26] God forbid someone be interested in justice at the Justice Department.

Senator Sheldon Whitehouse, Democrat of Rhode Island, a member of the Senate Judiciary Committee, said that "the Bush administration was engaged in a deliberate effort to inject partisan politics into the administration of justice." Whitehouse didn't mince words. In his words, these internships and programs "were made into a recruitment firm for conservatives, rewarding ideology with career advancement."[27]

It is suspected that this particular wave of bad judgment and obvious, egregious bias originated with the efforts of a notorious previously mentioned Gonzales protégée. I don't want to be too direct here, but I'll give you a hint: her initials are Monica Goodling. At least four officials at the Justice Department were named as either being directly in violation of the law or having "exercised poor judgment." When Justice folks were interviewed, quite a few of them pointed a finger at Ms. Goodling.[28]

It was Goodling who recommended a Ms. Esther Slater McDonald to be hired as counsel to acting Associate Attorney General William Mercer in June 2006. (Ms. McDonald, by the way, graduated from law school in 2003.) Goodling's charge then rose to becoming one third of a three-person committee that decided which applicants would be interviewed for internships and honors positions. She followed in Goodling's, and Gonzales's, footsteps, duly weeding out the applicants who didn't appear to be strictly Bushian.

McDonald was found out after a few other folks at Justice noticed their candidates weren't faring so well in the hiring process. In what has become a time-honored tradition in the Bush Justice Department, she made a hasty exit in October 2008, a day before she was scheduled to be interviewed by investigators.[29]

Obama Attorney General Eric Holder faces an uphill climb as he sorts through the wreckage of the Bush Justice Department. Fortunately, you couldn't find a man whose record and experience contrasts more with Gonzales. Attorney General Holder has long been a vocal proponent for the rule of law, a concept foreign to the Bush administration.

Culture War

Republicans were just supposed to talk a pretty good game about the culture war, but then they actually stepped out and started to fight the thing and now people hate them for it. What Bush started in 2000 was a two-election trick that had met its natural and timely death by 2008. Its utility was long exhausted. (Exhibit A in the sizable bank of evidence testifying to the demise of the culture war is the failure of John McCain's Hail Mary pick of one Governor Sarah Palin as his running mate.)

A favorite institution of mine, Media Matters, undertook a major report on Americans' political ideology. They used American National Election Studies from the University of Michigan and the University of Chicago and threw in data from Pew and Gallup, nonpartisan public opinion research resources, for good measure. The conclusion? Media Matters's "The Progressive Majority" report reads: "As all the data presented in this report make clear, whatever Americans choose to call themselves, on issue after issue—economic, social, security, and more—majorities of the public find themselves on the progressive side. And on many of the most contentious 'culture war' issues, the public has been growing more progressive year after year. The news media may not have noticed, but the facts are too clear to ignore."[30]

Professor Larry Bartels of Princeton, whose wisdom and work I lean on heavily in my chapter on the economy, wrote the following: "Do working class 'moral values' trump economics? No. Social issues (including abortion) are less strongly related to party identification and presidential votes than economic issues are, and that is even more true for whites in the bottom third of the income distribution than for more affluent whites."[31]

In the case that you may be uncomfortable with the Ivy League's pronouncements on working-class voters, which would be eminently reasonable, I'll turn to the west coast, to Professor Morrison Fiorina of Stanford: "In sum, observers of contemporary American politics have apparently reached a new consensus around the proposition that old disagreements about economics now pale in comparison to new divisions based on sexuality, morality, and religion. . . . Yet research indicates otherwise. . . . There is no culture war in the United States; no battle for the soul of America rages, at least none that most Americans are aware of."[32]

The Republicans committed too deeply to a strategy of playing off a supposed culture war. I'll give them this: in 2004, the culture war won them the election. They framed Kerry carefully, and they made sure to get their voters out. John Kerry was an effete, northeastern liberal, and they put the gay rights amendment on every state ballot and deployed every megachurch member they could reach. But that's over and done, and it's not going to work again. It's cashed out. As I've said before, and my friends Larry Bartels and Morrison Fiorina now say somewhat more elegantly, it's the economy, stupid.

The consequence of the Republicans' lingering preoccupation with the culture war is that it has led them to become a party of ridiculous positions. I don't want to say that I think Republicans are ridiculous people. I don't think that John McCain is a ridiculous man per se. But I think that intelligent design and creationism are ridiculous theories. And I use the word "theories" loosely. These positions are silly, and goofy, and, by the way, they don't make any sense. Yet the Republican Party has backed itself into a corner, and it is stuck saying Americans should learn these things in school. That shows how ridiculous the party has become.

With a recession and two wars, the Republicans had to be crazy to think that whatever minority of the country still agreed with them on the cultural issues was going to get them elected. Republicans would have to be certifiable to ever attempt a culture war strategy again. (Of course, that's not to say I hope they won't. I certainly hope to see the Republicans dedicate themselves enthusiastically to this strategy for another few election cycles.)

I go through the electoral limitations of relying on the Christian far right as a voting bloc in another chapter, but here's a quick summary analogy. Let's say you wanted to buy into a company. You went in and commissioned a study to see who was buying that company's product and would they fit into the prospects of long-term growth for that company. That's a cold, hard decision that people have to make every day if they want to be a part of something. Now look at the Republicans. Their prime consumers of their product are white people over sixty-five. Let's take whites over sixty-five as a percentage of the electorate. It was 90 percent when Carter ran, and it was 74 percent this year. Their basic base is a rapidly shrinking market share; the Christian right is shrinking. Not only that, the Republicans, McCain specifically, just aren't gassing up the Christian right like Bush did.

If politics were football, it'd be like the Republicans ran a post-pattern and are waiting in the end zone, but their quarterback got sacked a long time ago.

CHAPTER 2

TOD on GOP

The contradictions within the Republican party are visible on the surface and, in the view of Democrats, have delightfully led to all manner of internecine hand-wringing. The evangelical Christian and social conservatives find themselves in a marriage of convenience (does this violate a marriage's sanctity?) with economic conservatives, who in turn wonder about the single-minded obsession of the national security–focused conservatives. Consider it as the Pat Robertson Republicans versus the Rockefeller Republicans versus the Reagan Republicans. All represent different wings of the party and, as you might guess, a bird with three wings does not fly so well.

—JAMES CARVILLE, *FINANCIAL TIMES,* MAY 5, 2008

I'm going to go back to November 2000. I don't want to be a pedant, but this is important. November 2000 was the month that the entire strategy and underpinnings of the Bush presidency were set into place by a now infamous memo by Matthew Dowd that I mentioned earlier. To refresh your memory, dear reader, in that ignominious memo Dowd concluded that there was no more center, and that the Bush administration could govern and campaign from the right.

With few exceptions classic political strategy until that time, as practiced by literally every consultant and candidate, was simply this: move your candidate as far to the center as possible without alienating your base voters. Your task was to moderate your candidate's positions without turning off the voters most likely to be for you. Political scientists call it the Median Voter theorem. I call it common sense.

In 1992, for example, on the Clinton campaign, our first paid television commercial was on welfare reform. That commercial was a signal that Clinton was a new kind of Democrat. He was a pro–capital punishment, pro–welfare reform candidate, with the political dexterity to defend those positions while holding together the Democratic coalition.

George H. W. Bush said he wanted a kinder, gentler America. It wasn't subtle. His message was a blatant appeal to the people in the middle and a forerunner of his son's flirtation with 2000-era "compassionate conservatism."

These are all perfect examples of someone trying to move to the center while feverishly working to retain base voters.

With Dowd's memo, strategic doctrine in the Bush presidency shifted radically. The Bush camp began to operate on the belief that the center no longer existed, and they determined to govern, if it's not too strong a word, ruthlessly, from the right. Dowd had concluded that as long as they could keep the right jacked up, they could win elections, and Bush bought his thesis hook, line, and sinker.

In two election cycles, Dowd and Rove's strategy worked brilliantly. But it's like the classic story where someone sells his soul for temporary gain and ends up in hell for eternity. Dowd, Rove, and Bush made a deal with the devil. They traded victories in 2002 and 2004 for the future of the Republican Party.

Early on, it appeared McCain had taken heed and would stick to campaigning as a maverick. Then in late spring and early summer 2008, McCain went hard right—and later hard negative—in response to his slide in the polls. Every step McCain took toward Bush and Rove's Dowd-steered strategy grew Obama's margin over McCain.

The best authority on how McCain's decision to recycle Dowd's strategy helped sink his campaign is, well, Matthew Dowd. In

March, David Paul Kuhn published then-defected Dowd's quote that McCain "has sided himself so closely to the administration, especially on Iraq, now having various Bush advisers—that doesn't sit well with the public."[1]

America may be a divided country today, but it is most decidedly not an evenly divided country. It is becoming less and less an evenly divided country. If this were sports, I'd say, let's go to the videotapes—in politics, we say, let's go to the polls. So, here's my take on the death of the Republican Party, as supported at appropriate intervals by surveys and other forms of opinion measurement.

The Evidence: Republicans in Crisis

We already know that Bush was, to put it mildly, spectacularly unpopular. That's why reminders of John McCain's habit of voting with George W. Bush 90 percent of the time were a consistent, and successful, component of Obama's strategy last year.

What seems to be escaping notice is just how serious the problems of the Republican Party as a whole are for the long term. It's not just a Bush thing, and it's not just about Republicans' prospects in 2010, 2012, or 2014. I'll review the impact of the youth blowback later, when we discuss youth voters. For now, let's stick to the overview.

Republicans know they tapped out their base strategy by 2006. An article by Tod Lindberg in the *Weekly Standard* in 2006 explained Republican strategy:

> The electoral strategy the 1994 results invited was the one Karl Rove successfully exploited in three elections before stumbling badly in the fourth this year: The way to win elections is to find your people and get them to the polls. The premise is that "your people" are out there in sufficient numbers to produce victories, given a technically competent effort to turn them out. You

win elections not through conspicuous efforts to reach out to the middle to persuade undecided voters, who probably don't pay much attention to politics anyway. Rather, you focus your efforts on "your people."[2]

Now the Republicans have done a thorough job of making sure they don't have "people." In every election year as the election approaches, people take sides. In 2008, Americans weren't really taking sides. They were taking side.

In the fall of 2007, 40 percent of Americans identified themselves as independents in Gallup polls. By spring 2008, we saw the number of independents start to shrink. In June, only 36 percent thought of themselves as independent. In most years, polls show a rise in the party identification of *both* parties as independents take a stance. But in 2008, independents' defection wasn't what we'd call evenly distributed—from fall 2007 to June 2008, Democratic Party identification rose by 5 points while Republicans didn't claim a single convert.[3]

In Step with Bush,
Out of Step with the American People

McCain kept trying to claim he was a "Change" Republican. I don't really know what that would mean. But I didn't buy it. Neither did other Americans. McCain was the same as Bush and, although I didn't think I'd ever be able to say this, even worse on some points. We'll do a quick review of some of the worst of the Republican policies McCain regurgitated last year on the campaign trail because 2008 won't be the last time you see them and, dear reader, I'd like you to be prepared for the next Republican masquerading as Change who throws up these same talking points.

On Iraq, McCain parroted Bush. For months the McCain campaign Web site actually read that McCain wanted to send *more* troops to Iraq. Everyone has a different notion of how to solve Iraq.

There are senators who think we should draw down slowly, pundits who say we should just get out, wonks who say that Iraq should be divided into several states, and a strong and sane majority favoring some kind of timeline or timetable for U.S. presence in Iraq. Senator McCain is nowhere to be found in any of these reasonable categories or groups.

Let's review a few of the statements that were the rhetorical nails in the McCain campaign coffin. McCain said it would be fine if the United States spent one hundred years in Iraq.[4] The good senator from Arizona said it wasn't "too important" when the troops come home.[5] Of course, we're lucky he realizes we're in Iraq—he also couldn't keep Shiites and Sunnis straight without Joe Lieberman's help.[6]

Americans get it, but McCain suffers from a fundamental misapprehension of what's going on in the Middle East. This is the guy who said we could "muddle through Afghanistan"[7] and that we'd be "greeted as liberators" in Iraq. If that phrase sounds familiar, it's because Dick Cheney used the same one.[8]

McCain also followed in Bush's footsteps on the economy during one of the worst economic crises of the last one hundred years. Simply put, John McCain converted to the Republican religion of stealing from the poor to give to the rich. Back in 2001, McCain opposed Bush's tax cuts, saying they were "generous tax relief to the wealthiest individuals of our country at the expense of lower- and middle-income American taxpayers."[9] Now he's for Bush's billionaire-friendly tax cuts. As the saying goes, there's no one more zealous than a convert.

In fact, McCain felt so strongly about doing his part to relieve the plight of the upper-middle-class and rich American that he pledged to extend Bush's tax cuts on the campaign trail. The price tag on McCain's tax proposals was $2 trillion.[10] That means John McCain asked the American people to shell out $2 trillion for tax cuts for the wealthy and corporations—the top five oil companies would get almost $4 billion in tax breaks,[11] while the top ten health insurance companies would get about $2 billion[12]—even while spending $200 million *a day* in Iraq.[13]

What McCain's tax proposals made brilliantly clear to Americans is that, like Bush and the rest of the Republican Party, McCain doesn't really "get" economics. Actually, let me refine that statement: McCain doesn't even understand arithmetic.

McCain tried to sell his economic plan by telling folks that eliminating earmarks would cover the costs. In America According to the Republicans, the funds he would save from being thrown away on frivolous projects like bridges and hospitals would fund his tax breaks for the hardworking millionaires and corporate giants of America.

The first and most obvious problem with McCain's promise to cut all earmarks was the simple fact that earmarks do some good. Earmarks do things like keep Israel afloat, provide our veterans with housing, and fund critical medical research.[14] (One might also observe that Senator McCain had a bad habit of turning up to give speeches in places that have received earmarks.)[15]

The second issue, and this is where McCain's arithmetic really started to stink, was the claim that he could wring $65 billion out of the budget by cutting earmarks.[16] He could not, under even the broadest and most generous definition of what an earmark is, find $65 billion in earmarks.[17]

The third glaring error in McCain's reasoning would be the fact that $65 billion wouldn't even come close to bankrolling his tax breaks and corporate welfare plan. Given that the fine points of economics are not my strength, I'll direct you to Robert Gordon and James Kvaal of the Center for American Progress Action Fund, who exposed McCain's faulty calculus with embarrassing ease:

> The three sets of measures identified by McCain as potential revenue sources . . . would pay for only about 40 percent of McCain's proposals. First, eliminating absolutely all earmarks, without funding any of the projects elsewhere, would yield only $18 billion, according to Taxpayers for Common Sense. Second, eliminating and deeply cutting every program on a White House list of targeted programs . . . would yield $18 billion more (including heavy cuts in after-school programs, student

aid, public broadcasting, and job training). Third, the corporate tax breaks that McCain is considering eliminating would
yield only another $45 billion, according to the *Wall Street
Journal. . . .* Even in the highly unlikely event that McCain succeeded in obtaining all the savings that he is said to be
considering, he would need to make up more than $100 billion
per year in revenue. These funds would have to come from unprecedented cuts in Social Security or discretionary spending.

The Carville translation is this: McCain couldn't pay for his tax
breaks without screwing over American families.

Discretionary spending, by the way, is antiseptic Washington
jargon for the money the government spends on the services
and programs that help Americans, from education to housing to
medical research.[18] I don't have to explain to anyone how important Social Security is. Anyone with parents, grandparents, or the
intention of living past the age of sixty-five is in favor of Social
Security.

The health care plan McCain proposed was unapologetically
Bushian. Two reporters at the *New York Times* wrote dryly, "[Mc-
Cain's] proposal to move away from employer-based coverage was
similar to one that President Bush pushed for last year."[19] *The
Washington Post* likewise reviewed McCain's plan as "a market-
based solution with an approach similar to a proposal put forth by
President Bush last year."[20]

Here's the view of Republican proposals on health care from
30,000 feet: the annihilation of the employer-based health care system,[21] a tax credit that won't cover health insurance to start with
and won't keep up with rising health care costs,[22] and almost no
oversight or protections.[23] Right now, 158 million Americans get
health care through their employers. McCain proposed eliminating tax breaks for employers providing health insurance to their
workers.[24] Instead, McCain and his Republican cohort wanted to
give single people a $2,500 tax credit and families only $5,000.[25]

Math isn't my field, but I feel compelled to crunch a few numbers. According to the Kaiser Family Foundation, the most popular employer-provided health insurance plans cost the employer almost $12,000 a year.[26] Again, I'm not a mathematician, but by my estimates, taking $5,000 from $12,000 leaves $7,000. That's $7,000 a year that Americans are going to have to cover themselves. And $12,000 a year is optimistic. If $12,000 is the best bargain big employers can strike, just imagine what happens when they're out of the picture.

It is a self-evident truth that I have a soft spot for tough, smart women, and there are few women, or people, tougher or smarter than Elizabeth Edwards. She got it right on the Republicans' 2008 health care plan. I'm just going to turn it over to Mrs. Edwards to explain why it is that tossing people into the individual market is, to put it mildly, unconscionable: "Senator McCain's never been in the individual market, he doesn't know how difficult it is, in fact how impossible it is, if you happen to be one of the unlucky Americans who has a preexisting condition. He does, Senator McCain does. I do. Among the people who are employed right now and getting their insurance that way, fifty-six million of them do, and they're going to find it incredibly expensive, if it's available at all, for those people who have preexisting conditions."

Republicans don't seem to understand that there are only two kinds of people: sick, and not-yet-sick. The individual market doesn't work out for either type. You may be fine for a while if you're young and healthy. But as Benjamin Franklin said, only death and taxes are inevitable. And before we die, most of us get sick. Once you're sick, which we call "a preexisting condition" in Washington, getting insured in the individual market is at best difficult and at times impossible.

A few more numbers, here, and then I promise I'm done until the chapter on the economy. McCain said he'd increase his health care tax credit at the rate of inflation. That's a classic example of Republicans trying to make the absurd sound reasonable. Health care costs rise about 7 percent every year, and inflation rises only 2 percent. The cost of health care would rise quite a bit faster than the size of Republicans' already insufficient tax credit. By the calculations of my friends at the Center for American Progress, "In 2009, McCain's credit [would] cover 36% of the costs of an average family premium, by 2018 it would only cover 24%."[27]

The truth is simply this: McCain lined up behind Bush on every major policy issue, and that compounded his already unenviable problem of being a Republican in 2008. All the post-election analysis and policy jargon I can throw at you about how McCain hugged Bush couldn't make this point stronger than McCain and Bush did. McCain said that he "totally" supported Bush on the "transcendent issues," which could convince even the most reluctant of holdouts that McCain would continue Bush's policies.[28] (If that's not strong enough for you, there's always McCain's ill-conceived statement that Bush "has earned our admiration and love" in 2004.)[29]

Bush wanted Americans to elect McCain, in itself perhaps the most damning argument against McCain. Americans heard Bush saying McCain was the best choice to "carry forth his agenda,"[30] and Bush's promise that "If my showing up and endorsing him helps him—or if I'm against him and it helps him—either way, I want him to win."[31] That may be my favorite remark by George Bush on the topic of his own unpopularity. Even Bush knew that his endorsement of McCain was going to hurt McCain.

Americans had enough of Bush, and they weren't going to elect the guy who presented himself as his successor both substantively and rhetorically. In May 2008, 43 percent of voters said McCain would be too closely aligned with the Bush agenda.[32] By June, 49 percent told Gallup that they worried McCain would be too similar to Bush.[33] As McCain hugged Bush closer, the number kept climbing.

Just look at *The Washington Post* survey in May 2008. Let me offer a refresher: in May 2008, the Democratic primary was at its nastiest and most vicious. There were not more than a handful of populated places in the country where you could walk more than a few feet without hearing or seeing something about how the Democrats were attacking one another. (It was ugly, but none of this is to say that the Democratic primary this year was in any way close to being one of the nastiest elections I've witnessed in my lifetime—it was downright polite, if you ask me.)

So, going back to May 2008, even as the Democrats were nearly neck-and-neck and McCain was sitting pretty, Americans told *The Washington Post* that Obama, not McCain, would be more likely to bring change, had a better personality and temperament, better understood Americans, and had a clearer vision for the future. And when I say that people said Obama would be better on these things, I don't mean that a few more people preferred him—I mean that almost six in ten people thought that Obama would be better than McCain on all of these things, and only about three in ten gave McCain higher marks on any one of these things.[34]

For more on the demographic and analytical evidence of imminent Republican decline, I'll share with you the following memo.

To: James Carville
From: Rebecca Buckwalter-Poza
Re: Demographics and the Decline of the Republican Party

You've indicated that your sense of the election was that Democrats were doing better with those voters whose vote share was increasing, and that the Republicans were stuck with people like yourself—and by that I mean, old and white. You know, even a broken clock is right twice a day.

With few exceptions, it is true today that growing demographics are Democratic, and shrinking demographics are Republican. Republican base groups—most notably, white men and the Christian right—are decreasing as a share of the electorate, and the Republican Party is becoming a regional party.[35] Meanwhile, Democrats are benefiting from growing diversity and from the support of youth, who are overwhelmingly Democratic and increasingly politically engaged.

Bye, Bye, Bubba

The American public is growingly diverse, with more names like mine, and white men—like you—are no longer the king-makers of presidential politics. Mid-twentieth century, white men made up half of the electorate.[36] In 2008, white men made up only 36 percent of the electorate—barely more than a third—and their vote share is dropping by a percentage point a year.[37]

Republicans' margin among white men also slimmed signifi-cantly in 2008. While McCain defeated Obama among white male voters by 16 points, Obama improved on the Bush-Kerry margin by 9 points for the strongest showing of a Democratic presidential candidate among white male voters since Jimmy Carter in 1976.

Fall of the Christian Far Right

Over the past few decades Republicans have come to rely heav-ily on, and cater to, the Christian right as a key voting bloc, but they now face a problem we might term diminishing electoral returns. After taking a hard right to win the Christian right, Republicans have now maxed out support in a shrinking demo-graphic. In the 1950s, about four in five voters were married white Christians. Now only two in five voters are married, white, and Christian.[38]

Initially, the GOP's near monopoly on the Christian right was a tremendous asset. Alan Abramowitz of Emory University writes, "In American politics today, whether you are a married white Christian is a much stronger predictor of your political preferences than your gender or your class." The Republicans reaped electoral benefits from their steady inroads into the married white Christian demographic over the past forty or fifty years:

The Republican Party has been able to maintain and even slightly increase its share of the electorate since the 1960s by steadily increasing its support among married white Christians . . . between the 1950s and the first decade of the 21st century, Republican identification among married white Christians increased by more than 20 percentage points, going from about 40 percent to over 60 percent. . . . Between the 1970s and the first decade of the 21st century, Republican identification among conservative married white Christians increased by 26 points, going from 64 percent to 90 percent.[39]

There's nowhere to go from 90 percent, and Republicans aren't winning moderate and liberal Christians. While they were increasing their margin among conservative married white Christians, Republicans stalled out with moderate and liberal Christians. Since the 1950s, Republicans increased party identification among the moderates by only 5 points, to 43 percent, and they slipped by 10 points with the liberals, to 13 percent.[40]

The shrinking Christian right leaves a void in the Republicans' collection of base groups—and they can't look to any growing groups to replace those votes.

Republicans as a Regional Party

The Republican Party now relies heavily on a few regions for all of its seats in Congress. Of the 41 Republican-held Senate seats, 20 are southern, and of 178 Republican House seats, 86 are in the South. Nearly half of the Republican Party's representatives in Congress come from the South (48.4 percent). Moreover, Republicans' strength in regional strongholds is slipping. In 2008, Republicans lost advantages in party identification in the industrial Midwest and farm states and held leads in only two regions of the country, the South and the mountain states, by less than 2 points each.[41]

Latinos Rising

Latino and Hispanic voters increased their vote share by a percentage point from 2004, from 8 to 9 percent, representing an increase of hundreds of thousands of votes—that went primarily to Obama. In three battleground states—Colorado, Nevada, New Mexico—Latinos increased their vote share by 5 points or more. Nationwide, Latinos voted for Obama by a margin of 36 percent—67 percent to 31 percent for McCain. In Florida, a state where Latinos have traditionally voted Republican, Obama won 57 percent of the Latino vote.[42]

African-American Turnout

In 2004, African-Americans made up 11 percent of the electorate. Four years later, they accounted for 13 percent of all voters in the presidential election. The 2-point increase in vote share is tremendous. The U.S. Census Bureau will likely find in 2010 that African-American turnout rates surpassed white turnout rates for the first time.[43]

The Rise of Multiethnic, Multiracial, Multilingual, Overwhelmingly Democratic Young Voters

Young Americans are dramatically Democratic and newly politically active. In 2008, voters ages eighteen to twenty-four gave Obama a 38-point margin, 68 percent to just 30 percent for McCain. The margin was slightly larger among voters age twenty-five to twenty-nine, who broke 69 to 29 (40 points) for Obama.[44] Youth also called themselves Democrats in much greater numbers, giving Democrats a 19-point advantage in party identification.

Turnout among eighteen- to twenty-nine-year-olds rose between 4 and 5 percentage points from 2004—and was 11 points higher than in 2000.[45] Attempts to undercut the impact of the youth vote mistakenly cite the 1 percent increase in young people's share of the electorate from 2004 to 2008 as unremarkable. One percent of the total electorate—when more than 131 million votes were cast this year—represents more than 1 million votes.

Contrary to Republican claims, a great body of evidence proves that, once established, patterns of voting remain consistent. Rather than aging out of their Democratic leanings, these young people will continue to vote Democratic over the course of their lifetime.

The youngest generation of voters is multiethnic, multiracial, and multilingual, and future generations will be even more diverse. Last year, 11 percent of young voters identified themselves as Latino (as compared with 6 percent overall), and 19 percent said they were black (as compared with 13 percent of all voters).[46] According to the Census Bureau, 33 percent of children under eighteen are ethnic or racial minorities. One in five youth under eighteen is an immigrant or the child of an immigrant.[47] Increasing diversity likely translates to further Democratic gains. In 2008, 96 percent of African-Americans and 67 percent of Latinos voted for Obama.[48]

The Republican Party in 2009

Republicans are reeling in the wake of the 2008 elections. Republicans lost House seats, Senate seats, the presidency, and have the lowest political brand in the history of polling. That set of facts calls for finger-pointing, and it calls for a blame game. There's plenty of blame to go around. Republicans have been branded by the legacy of a disastrous war and an unprecedented financial crisis. That's not to mention the fact that the single most prominent member of their party may prove to be the most unpopular president in U.S. history.

Despite themselves, Republicans nominated the best possible candidate last year—a year in which Republicans were about as popular as a root canal. (If possible, they are even less popular now.) Yet the Republicans couldn't get what's left of their base to rally behind McCain, proving that the modern GOP is now a regionalized, extreme party that can't succeed without satisfying the far right and the Christian right.

In July 2008, fewer than six in ten conservatives supported McCain.[49] That doesn't sound too bad, so let's get a little perspective on it. In 2004, Bush carried 87 percent of conservatives. That means that, as of July 2008, McCain lagged 29 points behind Bush's 2004 performance among conservatives.[50] In the 2008 election, Republican turnout actually dropped. According to Curtis Gans of American University's Center for the Study of the American Electorate, "Republican turnout declined by three percentage points to 25 percent of the electorate. The six-point advantage the Democrats had in the eligible vote was the largest since the Lyndon Johnson landslide against Barry Goldwater in 1964—8.8 percentage points. Republican turnout declined in 44 states and the District of Columbia and increased in only six—none by a greater amount than two percentage points."

The lead of a *New York Times* article on November 7, 2008, maintained: "President-elect Barack Obama succeeded in chiseling off small but significant chunks of white evangelical voters who have been the foundation of the Republican Party for decades, a close look at voting patterns reveals."[51]

The truth is, McCain never managed to mobilize the white evangelical voters critical to Bush's victory in 2004. They were crazy about Bush, but indifferent to McCain. Only 10 percent of white evangelical Christians said they were excited by the election, compared with 20 percent of Americans overall.[52] So here's the matchup:

McCain 2008 vs. Bush 2004. In 2004, Bush won 78 percent of white evangelicals.[53] In 2008, McCain won 74 percent of white evangelicals. That means McCain came in 4 points behind Bush's 2004 level of support from white evangelicals. Considering that the Republican Party has been relying upon and steadily building support among white evangelicals for decades, this backsliding signals serious trouble for the GOP.

With demographics against him, it was crucial that McCain be able to energize all of his shrinking base. But McCain just couldn't get people excited—even with his Hail Mary pick of Sarah Palin as his running mate, which was, admittedly, probably a smart move so far as mobilizing the Republican base goes.

Here I'll take a moment to address Governor Palin. Although, again, I think she was a predictable pick by a desperate Republican Party: Sarah Palin is uniquely unqualified to hold the office to which she aspired. One might remember that I did go so far as to show a picture of Wasilla's City Hall on air while commenting on CNN. It looks just like a Louisiana bait shop. The Katie Couric interviews left me speechless. They might have been the worst interviews in the history of television. The story of Sarah Palin is this: she was exposed as what she is, incompetent.

I found the Palin-inspired post-campaign finger-pointing within the McCain camp to be both intriguing and entertaining. I've heard more than a few people who ought to know better ask, was the Republicans' loss Sarah Palin's fault?

The McCain campaign and, indeed, much of the Republican Party, being literally exhausted from defending itself from every right-wing blowhard and Bush lackey in the country, did decide to blame Sarah Palin for circumstances beyond their, and her, control. (Namely, the crash of the Republican brand.)

Governor Palin, who may not have learned much in her run for national office but learned enough to participate in the blame game, got her finger out and pointed it right back. And so we have Palin doing interviews with Matt Lauer in her kitchen and deliciously vicious stories ranging from her appearing for meetings in her hotel room wrapped in a towel (somewhat believable) to not knowing the countries of North America (100 percent believable) to not knowing Africa was a continent (95 percent believable). The campaign shouted, screamed, and cried to anyone who would listen about how Palin didn't read and didn't prepare for her interviews or the debate.

Even if all of that's true, let's go back to the main point here: no one could have overcome the incompetence of the Bush administration. Nothing could have made the shrinking base the Republicans now depend upon suddenly an electoral force capable of securing a victory for McCain. Contemporary American conservativism is an accumulation of reactionary, pseudopopulist, intellectually devoid whiners, xenophobes, racists, and Luddites.

For every step McCain took to try to unify conservatives, he lost crucial swing voters. Although initially popular, Sarah Palin ultimately became an albatross around McCain's neck. Obama beat McCain among independents by 8 points, 52 to 44 percent—even as the pool of independents became more conservative.

Every four years, the number of independents shrinks as the presidential election approaches. Usually the gains to each party are roughly even; but in 2008, independents moved toward the Democrats, and Republicans became independents. In polling terms, there was an increase in Democratic Party identification—and a small decrease in Republican Party identification. That should surprise no one. Who would really be moved to join the Republican Party by the events of the last year? On November 2, 2008, 38 percent of Americans identified as Democrats, 34 percent identified as independents, and only 26 percent admitted to being Republicans.[54]

In short, Republicans have no hope of making serious inroads into Democratic advantages in 2010, or likely 2012 or 2014 and so on. It's time to call TOD on the GOP.

WHY MCCAIN PICKED PALIN

Here's the scene: the top brains in the McCain campaign and whatever high-ranking Republicans get a say in such matters are in a room, and they're all very aware that they're going to lose the election. If they pick Pawlenty, Romney, Ridge, Crist, or any of the other oft-mentioned top contenders for the vice-presidential slot, it doesn't move any votes. They're getting ready to go to the convention, and they instinctively know that any of the conventional picks would (a) provide no additional chance to win; (b) ensure that what promised to be a lethargic convention would remain so. In the case of Ridge, they would probably have had walkouts.

This is a campaign that's looking for a shake-up-the-equation pick to fire up the base, preferably a Republican without Washington connections. Suddenly somebody or some bodies say, we have a brilliant idea: Sarah Palin. Consider the following, they say. Palin is a woman, so she'll cut into the women antagonized by Hillary, and she neutralizes our diversity problem. She's not from Washington—she's the governor of Alaska and she actually ran against corrupt Republicans. This is a woman who isn't just loved but revered by the Christian right, and she will fire up the party like you've never seen. They keep spinning. The governor is great in front of a camera. She's a former newsperson (and a beauty queen), and she understands the media.

At this point, 99 percent of people in politics would stop and say, this is a perfect story, and the Republicans have just met the woman of their dreams. And it was a dream at that point. Palin was the remedy for every problem they had: a lackluster convention, a depressed base, people hating Washington Republicans, a reputation for an old white guy party with an old white guy candidate, and a flagging maverick brand.

For those old white men in the room, the question was, why not? It seems to me that they skipped that part of the discussion.

People said, we can bring her up to speed. We can brief her.

Someone raises Troopergate and her tendency to abuse executive power in Alaska. The answer is easy: there was a deal with her brother-in-law and she stuck up for her sister. Who cares? If they knew at this point, they probably discussed the fact that the eldest Palin daughter was on her way to becoming a teenage mother. At that point they said, the right will love that. It's a choice families make every day. It humanizes her.

Their plan was to come out and own the narrative they created for this unknown political figure. At a level, it made so much sense it was ridiculous. It was a classic example of a father asking his daughter why she was walking into the house at eight in the morning. She replies, I fell asleep on the couch. It's up to the father whether he wants to let that go or investigate. Well, the Republican Party and the McCain campaign being the father in this situation, they wanted to believe Sarah fell asleep on the couch.

I almost understand it. From their point of view, what could they have imagined as the worst-case scenario? Who cared that she had no intellectual depth? That's the last thing that modern conservativism requires from anyone. It had become part of the tapestry of modern conservatism that stupidity was actually a virtue. That intellectualism and thought were things to be contemptuous of.

If you were a Republican or a conservative in the late summer or early fall of 2008, that woman was your dream. Sure, she didn't know anything about foreign policy and she didn't even have a passport until the year before. Of course she had no idea about any of the pressing national or international policy issues. But Republicans have come to embrace shallowness and lack of curiosity in their politicians. I actually think that a lot of people in the McCain campaign were encouraged by the fact that she was a simpleton.

Palin might even have a national political career in front of her still as long as there's a significant part of this country that values simpletons and believes that a solution to our problems can reside in a profoundly unthoughtful person. I would like to think we're never going to go back to that, that Bush has pretty much ended that strain of belief. But I am also keenly aware that American conservatism has reserved a big place at the table for the reactionary, thoughtless right-winger for the foreseeable future.

Time for a Fox-Hunt

Having reviewed the ridiculous positions the Republican Party has taken, let's look at how the Republicans do their best to convince Americans that their positions are valid and mainstream. (Or, in other words, it's time for a Fox-hunt.)

Over the course of decades Republicans have built an infrastructure that allows them to marshal everyone they've got, from elected officials to entire news networks (Fox), to create artificial uproars on cue, à la ACORN scandal that wasn't in 2008.

Analyzing Republicans' influence on the media is a kind of political "Are You Smarter Than a Fifth Grader?" Here's your test:

1. Is Fox fair and balanced, or is it Republican propaganda?

One of the frustrating things in Washington is that you're supposed to go around with a solemn face and argue things that are really not arguable. Among these non-argument arguments that we're expected to have, my favorite may be creationism. Naturally I also enjoy spending endless hours cornered in debates about global warming and whether Social Security works or not. (Of course it does.)

So we sit around and pontificate on silly-ass things that have been decided a long time ago. There comes a point at which the body of evidence is so conclusive, is so overwhelming, is so definitive that even unreasonable people don't attempt to make a contrary argument. For example, the earth is round, not flat. We accept that. There's no less evidence that the earth is warming, no less evidence that the earth is not 5,000 years old, but somehow or another, we scratch our chins and argue. An argument that fits into the creationism, global warming, flat-earth sphere of issues is the "objectivity" of Fox News.

Only a massive liar or blatant hypocrite would dare argue this point. Consider the following facts about Fox:

- Claimed WMDs were found and never retracted it
- Roger Ailes was former President George Herbert Walker Bush's chief media strategist
- SVP John Moody sent memos on how to advance conservative agenda in Fox News
- John Ellis chaired the Fox election desk in 2000
- A 2003 study showed that 80 percent of Fox viewers believed one of the following three falsehoods: Saddam behind 9/11; WMDs in Iraq; world supportive of Iraq War
- Even tried to call Mark Foley a Democrat after it was revealed he was initiating inappropriate contacts and communications with his underage male pages
- Said Obama was educated in a Muslim madrassa, although CNN later sent a reporter to the school, which was actually non-denominational and public
- When "Scooter" Libby was convicted of four of five felony counts, Fox ran the headline: "Libby Found Not Guilty of Lying to FBI"

2. Is Bill O'Reilly a reasonable, balanced source of news and analysis, or is he a staunch Bush defender who hasn't met a government policy he didn't like?

Fox News claims it's balanced. O'Reilly claims he's an independent. But as my friend Paul Begala says, "Don't pee on my boots and tell me it's raining." The audience, topics, and guests all ooze conservatism. (And "ooze" is a particularly appropriate word when we're talking about Republicans, to be clear.) For any viewer unpersuaded after a few minutes tuned to Fox, there's the set of explicit instructions propagated by Rupert Murdoch on the conservative vent and purpose of the network, and there's no getting around the fact that O'Reilly is as "red" as they come. When it comes to O'Reilly, the best evidence of his lunacy comes from O'Reilly himself.

Here's O'Reilly on global warming and the environment:

March 4, 2008: Responding to a viewer's email about whether the current global warming "scare" is "natural" or "man-made," Fox News' Bill O'Reilly asserted: "It's all guesswork." Contrary to O'Reilly's assertion, the United Nations Intergovernmental Panel on Climate Change has concluded that the Earth is warming and human activity is very likely responsible for most of that warming.[55]

Ready for more? Read on for Bill O'Reilly's sophisticated understanding of the complex social and economic mechanisms at work in creating poverty in this country:

It's hard to do it because you gotta look people in the eye and tell 'em they're irresponsible and lazy. And who's gonna wanna do that? Because that's what poverty is, ladies and gentlemen. In this country, you can succeed if you get educated and work hard. Period. Period.[56]

One might think there's a limit to the number of stupid things that can come from one individual's mouth, but Bill O'Reilly keeps proving me wrong. I'm thinking of a gem of a quote from O'Reilly circa January 2000 (see if you can spot the moment when O'Reilly realized what he was saying):

I don't understand why in the year 2000, with all of the media that we have, that a certain segment of the African-American community does not understand that they must aggressively pursue their child's welfare. That is they have to stop drinking, they have to stop taking drugs and boozing, and—and whites do it, too! Whites do it, too![57]

Here's Bill O'Reilly's sympathetic and well-reasoned take on the "Don't Ask, Don't Tell" policy, given July 7, 2000:

That's my advice to all homosexuals, whether they're in the Boy Scouts, or in the Army or in high school: Shut up, don't tell anybody what you do, your life will be a lot easier.[58]

And just to prove he's remarkably nasty, even for a far right nut job, and that's stiff competition, Bill O'Reilly on Arianna Huffington and the *Huffington Post*:

I don't see a difference between [Arianna] Huffington and the Nazis.

What's the difference between the Ku Klux Klan and Arianna Huffington?

There's no difference between what Huffington and Nazis do.

The whole [*Huffington Post*] is a sewer.[59]

Finally, because the irony of Bill O'Reilly protesting someone taking advantage of freedom of speech is just too ironic to ignore, here's O'Reilly proposing that we deny Americans protesting the war in Iraq their civil freedoms. Because nothing protects freedom and democracy like tossing Americans exercising their constitutional rights in jail.

You must know the difference between dissent from the Iraq war and the war on terror and undermining it. And any American that undermines that war, with our soldiers in the field, or undermines the war on terror, with 3,000 dead on 9/11, is a traitor. Everybody got it? Dissent, fine; undermining, you're a traitor. Got it? So, all those clowns over at the liberal radio network, we could incarcerate them immediately. Will you have that done, please? Send over the FBI and just put them in chains, because they, you know, they're undermining everything and they don't care, couldn't care less.[60]

3. Is Fox's reporting on the war in Iraq biased?

In 2008, it was discovered that the Bush White House had been manipulating coverage of the war in Iraq by giving select analysts tremendous access—and sending them on camera armed with Bush-approved talking points. As former Fox "news analyst" and retired Green Beret Robert S. Bevelacqua said, "It was them saying, 'We need to stick our hands up your back and move your mouth for you.' "[61] That's pretty much all Fox is, ever.

The Center for Excellence in Journalism studied the amount of time each news channel spent on coverage of the war in Iraq early in 2007. Fox spent half as much time as MSNBC, and significantly less than CNN. During the day, CNN could be counted on to spend a fifth of its time on Iraq, with MSNBC only slightly behind. Fox spent only 6 percent of its airtime covering the Iraq War.

Fox's clear Republican bias on Iraq isn't exactly a fluke. It's the tip of the iceberg. Let's check coverage of the Department of Justice fiasco. MSNBC used 8 percent of its airtime to cover the firings of Justice Department officials, and CNN was on it 4 percent of the time. Fox covered the firings during only 2 percent of the news cycle. That's only a little more than nine minutes in eight hours for a scandal with tremendous legal and political implications.[62]

The Republicans close ranks to try to defend Fox. Tim Graham of the conservative Media Research Center says that Fox focuses on American news, and it's more balanced in its coverage because it's showing both the positive and the negative side of the war in Iraq. Unlike the unwaveringly negative coverage on CNN and MSNBC, he argued, Fox's programs give both positive and negative coverage of the war.

Several glaring issues present themselves here. The first would be, how can the Iraq War not qualify as an American issue? We have thousands of Americans dead and more Americans set to die, and it's American funding and American resources that we're pouring into this war. It doesn't get much more American than that.

The second major problem with Mr. Graham's response is the fact that there's no balance to be had in coverage of the Iraq War. Between May 15 and July 21 of 2006, Fox gave twice as many positive accounts of the war as CNN and MSNBC.[63] Presumably, although Fox often seems to be off in its own world, all three networks were reporting on the same war. The total number of U.S. soldiers who had died in "Operational Iraqi Freedom" or "Operation Enduring Freedom" as of December 20, 2008, was 4,200. The total number of soldiers who had been wounded in action was more than 30,000. I can say for a fact these numbers are higher now, as you read this.

4. Is Fox that biased, really?

In short, yes. Only if you believe the earth is flat, 5,000 years old, and getting cooler could you believe Fox is a legitimate news network. If you believe the earth is round, millions of years old, getting warmer, and there weren't WMDs found in Iraq, then you don't.

Fox anchors and executives seem to think that if they click their heels three times and say "fair and balanced," it'll suddenly be true. Take these gems from Brit Hume:

> You know, we get a ton of email; everybody does now. It gives us a kind of a pulse that you can feel. What we hear people saying is thank you for being fair; thank you for being balanced. So my sense of that is that within the media world, among my colleagues, the conventional wisdom is we're a right-wing network. I don't accept that view, and I don't think our viewers do either.[64]

I'll save my speculation on the likely proportion of "thank-you" emails Brit Hume receives that were written by friends, family, and

Hume himself for later. For now, I'll just repeat a simple fact: saying it's true doesn't make it so.

Bill O'Reilly admitted that balance isn't the guiding principle of his show, ratings are. He complained in December 2006 that the lowest-rated portion of his talk show on the previous night was when he covered the Iraq War. The highest? The Britney Spears segment. Too bad Bill hasn't returned to entertainment news coverage.

I can hear the objection now. Brit Hume's saying, "Mr. Carville, you attacked Fox News as liars and hypocrites, but you come on our channel to promote your book." I have a reply ready. "Yes, Mr. Hume, that's right. I also went on the *Colbert Report*, although I don't believe anything Stephen says."

Why doesn't Fox just say it's a right-wing propaganda channel? Then I can sit back to watch it the same way I watch the *Colbert Report*. Not for coverage or news or facts. To laugh. For God's sake, man, don't sit there and tell me you're a credible news-gathering organization—you're not.

During the Democratic primary, it was clear to me and others that certain outlets had a pronounced bias against one Hillary Rodham Clinton. It was a perceptible, problematic, if somewhat understandable, bias. Yet that was nothing compared to Fox's severe ideological tilt, which is all the more vile for the fact that Fox refuses to admit that it is biased. By comparison, during the general election, *Politico*'s John Harris and Jim VanderHei, formerly of *The Washington Post*, examined charges of broad media bias against McCain and for Obama—and confirmed them.[65]

Not Just Fox

It's not just Fox that gets it wrong. (Although, generally, the difference between Fox and other news entities is that sometimes other news entities get it right.) Let's take the *New York Times*. If you need one statistic that shows the mentality of the twentieth-century mainstream media, here it is: the *New York Times* printed 588,903 words on the Whitewater scandal during the Clinton administration, and it spent only 395,472 words on the decision to go to war in Iraq in 2003.

The media has failed in its duty. The role of the journalist is, fundamentally, to analyze and report events. Not only is the media not covering the big stuff ("I hear there's something going on in the Middle East"), it's spending hours on celebrities and socialites. I shouldn't know who Paris Hilton is.

At least Paris is just wasted coverage. If the media would agree to do a good job on the big issues when they deign to cover them, that's a deal I could live with. But instead we see lazy reporting. Like *Time* throwing up a memo written by the McCain campaign during the election as an article on McCain's campaign strategy.[66]

Worse than laziness, there is now a pernicious tendency on the part of the media to represent two perspectives on an issue as equally legitimate, even when the vast weight of evidence and proof lies on one side. There aren't two sides to the global warming debate. There are many different strains of thought on how to solve the environmental crisis, but there are no two sides to the issue of global warming: it's happening, and it's caused by human activity. Need another example? One word: evolution.

The media is playing into the hands of the right by giving their hacks and shills credibility on these issues. I don't want to see another Sunday morning show seating a creationist sitting next to a Harvard professor or another *New York Times* article quoting a minister who says that abstinence-only education is a really effective way to teach our teens about their bodies. Evolution happened, and teenagers are going to have sex. (These are perhaps two of the most irrefutable facts of our existence.)

CHAPTER 3

Why the Republicans Got Spanked in 2008

We've made fun of Karl Rove and the Republicans for a couple of chapters, and now I'm about to give one of my classic long-winded lectures. To build on the win in November, there's a few issues Democrats have to be on top of, and there's a certain way we've got to talk about them.

You're probably saying, "We're in, we won. What could you possibly have to say, Carville?" There is always the risk of history repeating itself: we get voted in, we lock up, and it takes too long to get anything done. I've been screaming at the Democrats to get it together and get a narrative for so long it doesn't seem like there could be anything new for me to say on the topic. Stick with me, I do.

The narrative the Democrats are absolutely, indisputably positioned to develop and deliver following 2008 is the Real Deal. Republicans have been quite literally set on destroying the world. (Although now it could be argued they're more interested in destroying one another.) They've set us back years on basic domestic indicators like income and health care and they've sunk numerous government agencies. Every time I thought I'd come up with something the Bush administration couldn't screw up or didn't have time to screw up with all the other screwing up they were doing, a headline proved me wrong. I expect the revealing headlines and exposés will continue as the housecleaning proceeds. It would test the imagination to try to fathom what dark secrets the Bush

administration succeeded in sweeping under the rug in the Department of Justice or shelving in the basement of the Agriculture
Building.

There was a story by Eric Lipton in the *New York Times* in September 2007 that completely confirmed every fear I had about the
Bush administration. No, it wasn't about the economy per se or
even about the war in Iraq or some fool thing Bush said. It was
about RTVs and imported toys. Consumer product regulation under Bush was at an all-time low. In the 1970s, there were more than
1,000 employees at the Consumer Product Safety Commission. Toward the end of the Bush years, there were about 420. That marked
a 12.5 percent drop from 2000, even, by the way.

Cut to Gaithersburg, Maryland, September 2007. One man was
responsible for testing every toy reported to be dangerous in the
United States. His testing ground was a square foot behind the
door in the cramped laboratory to which the Bush administration
relegated the dwindling staff of testers. In Los Angeles, one woman
working part time was responsible for inspecting the 15 million
plus truck-size containers that come in through the port each
year.

Remember all those stories about toys and children's jewelry
imported from China that contained lead? Cuts in funding and staff
coincided with a surge in imports from China under Bush. Over
the past ten years, imports have risen from $62 billion to $246 billion. But in September 2007, only eighty-one employees were inspecting imports nationwide. Bush was actually reducing the
number of people looking after product safety as imports from
China and other countries with few or no regulations—and no
agreement to observe or even consider U.S. safety regulations, I
might mention—continued to grow.

Funding cuts decimated the agency, stripping it down to a budget of $62 million. That sounds like a lot, but, in context, it means
Bush left only $62 million to regulate an industry topping $1.4 trillion and rising. If the Bush administration had had its way, the
safety commission's budget would be nonexistent.[1]

Returning to the somewhat bigger picture, there's the war in Iraq. Bush and his crew of neocons left Obama to end a conflict that is going to affect not only the United States but all international relations for a century to come. Thousands of young American men and women are dead. Tens of thousands of Iraqi civilians have been killed not only in the invasion and civil war but at the hands of overzealous private contractors hired and let loose in Iraq by the U.S. State Department. Hundreds of billions of dollars have been spent—and more than a few billion lost[2]—in Iraq.

Obama and the Democrats want to save the world, quite literally. We are the authors of a narrative that is newly urgent, newly relevant, and newly positive. We're for the Real Deal, for pushing the policies that will meet the needs of our communities in the wake of eight disastrous years of the Bush administration.

Guess what else is new this time? It's not a narrative just about the things the Republicans have done wrong; it's about playing up what the Democrats have right. That's going to mean harnessing the energy and enthusiasm the Obama campaign generated and reminding the American public about Democrats' leadership on health insurance, an issue the Republicans have handily hung themselves on with last year's centerstage battle over S-CHIP (the State Children's Health Insurance Program), not to mention the environment and energy.

We've always been on the right side of environmental policy, one of the few policy areas we didn't somehow manage to hand over to the Republicans along with morality, family values, and security. There hasn't been a Republican since Nixon who's been right on the environment.

You can't escape the headlines and news stories testifying to the fact that the earth is warming. They're in your face every day. It's hurricane followed by hurricane followed by hurricane, punctuated by stories about runners dying from heat-related causes during marathons. If you manage to miss the headlines, just walk outside. Check the setting on your air conditioner. It's plain getting hotter.

Conservatives attempting to deny the onset of global warming attempt to cite how cool it was in 2008 as proof the earth isn't warming. That's so easy to refute it's sad. To go to the *Christian Science Monitor,* "the only reason that this year seemed so cold is that the rest of this decade has been so hot. . . . While it's true that 1998 was the hottest year on record, none of these commenters has mentioned that the next seven hottest years were, in order, 2005, 2003, 2002, 2004, 2006, 2007, and 2001, according to Britain's Met Office."[3]

Not convinced? Try *Time:* "Even though 2008 is cooler than the past several years, it's still likely to rank as the 10th warmest year since the beginning of climate records in the 1850s."[4]

Between global warming and the price of gas, we're also ready to drive home energy independence. Fossil fuels are finite, environmentally destructive, and now economically untenable. A few people are finally ready to trade in that SUV for a Prius.

Of course, it's not just policy Obama and the Democrats have to be able to talk about. We have to talk about the Bush administration, too, and it's necessary to understand exactly what it is that went so wrong. Remind folks of the positive and the good times ahead, but keep the lessons of the last eight years fresh if you want to kept the Democrats in office for forty years.

The searing critique of the Bush administration is that their politics were based in fantasy, not reality. They talked a big game, and they didn't come through for the American people. In fact, they left the country far worse off than it was before they got into office by every measure I know of. They didn't even really have a plan, real or unreal, for an occupation in Afghanistan or Iraq. Talk of supply-side economics and tax cuts for the wealthy did not translate into a more robust economy—quite the opposite.

As Bush left, the American people were left with the feeling that government had been engaged in a fantasy—a fantasy in foreign policy, environmental policy, and health care policy, and a fantasy in economic policy—that didn't involve them. Americans are still experiencing very real problems, problems that are mounting, as a consequence of the Republican's eight-year sideline trip into the realm of fantasy.

The lesson of 2008 was that Americans are willing to empower a political party that offers achievable, real solutions to problems that are much more evident to the average American than they are to the elites residing in government. So, let's respond to that, and let's go out and spank the Republicans again and again.

CHAPTER 4

Katrina: The Failures of Republican-Run Government

What happened in New Orleans was not an act of God. It was an act of negligence. The levees were supposed to withstand storms much larger than Katrina, and they broke. In the days after Katrina, the government failed the people of the Gulf again and again. Katrina was one of the central events that shattered the public's confidence in Bush and the Republican Party, a fact that even Bush aides admitted as Bush was leaving office in December 2008.[1]

Thousands of people suffered in the days and months following Katrina. People suffered, and died, because the Bush administration underfunded and disempowered a critical government agency. A total of 378,000 people were displaced after the hurricane, forced to find other places to live throughout the country.[2] The rash of incompetence that began at 1600 Pennsylvania Avenue had an impact that's still evident on every street in the Lower Ninth Ward today.

To some, Katrina may now seem a distant memory, a current event turned historical footnote. But it has been nearly four years since the levees broke, yet large portions of New Orleans still have not been repaired. Critical services have not been restored, and many people still have not been able to return home. Any American surprised by the Bush administration's failures in Baghdad should be forcibly marched aboard a flight to New Orleans, which is still only slowly recovering.

I include this chapter for several reasons. The first is to expose and debunk the Bush administration's lies and failures, both of which are very relevant to the thesis of this book. The second is to put in writing my thoughts on the topic, which I have rarely had the opportunity to share in full elsewhere. It is unthinkable to me to write a book on the American political landscape in 2009 that does not stop to examine what Katrina and the days that followed meant for the people of the Gulf—and what those days said about the Republican Party and their philosophy of government.

The bulk of this chapter is made up of a fact-based timeline, the final word on the Bush administration's shortcomings in Louisiana and Mississippi. For a more personal understanding, I ask you to skip to the end of the book and consider the story of my friend, a Katrina survivor who returned to New Orleans after thirteen months in Dallas. Everyone tries to articulate what happened in one way or another, with numbers or charts or maps, but his story truly is the best way to tell the story of New Orleans during and after Katrina.

The story of Katrina is a chronology of incompetence that began on January 4, 2001, even before that miserable day that George Bush was sworn into office.

At the same press conference where he announced Karl Rove's appointment as a senior White House adviser, George Bush appointed Joe Allbaugh to head the Federal Emergency Management Agency (FEMA). At the event announcing the appointment, Bush admitted, "FEMA is an incredibly important part of a president's team. The person who runs FEMA is someone who must have the trust of the president. Because the person who runs FEMA is the first voice, oftentimes, [that] someone whose life has been turned upside down hears from."[3]

You'd think after speaking those words, George Bush would ap-point someone who had spent a lifetime working in disaster management; instead, he hired a Republican hack.

Let us review Joe Allbaugh's qualifications for earning "the trust of the president" to run FEMA. Allbaugh began his work as a Republican operative at a young age, volunteering for Barry Goldwater's campaign at twelve.[4]

After serving on Republican campaigns and in Republican administrations, Joe managed George Bush's campaign for governor in 1994 and served as his chief of staff in Texas. Then, in 1999, he managed George Bush's campaign for the White House. (That's as close as he came to an emergency management job.) It should come as no surprise that many FEMA veterans didn't like the fact that Allbaugh had almost no experience managing disasters and disaster relief. The Bush administration was, not uncharacteristically, unmoved by the objections of the competent.

Allbaugh took control of FEMA and did exactly what you would expect a Republican political operative to do. He began to privatize the functions of the agency, giving juicy contracts to large corporations along the way. Now, Joe doesn't deserve all the blame for this. After all, he was following orders.

One of the first initiatives George Bush undertook when he became president was a government-wide effort to end government, working hard to hand off vital services to the lowest bidder. Bush was bold. He even handed out big-dollar contracts without a bid under the heading of "cost plus." Meaning if the company spent a dollar, the government would pay them $1.05. The reasonably intelligent might point out that this arrangement incentivizes companies to spend more than necessary to complete projects. No one in the Bush administration seemed to object.

When it comes to emergency management, picking the lowest bidder saves money, but it costs lives.

Actual disaster response experts were not pleased with this announcement that was sure to make their lives more difficult. William Waugh of Georgia State University, who had done work for FEMA pre-Bush, pointed out, "Pretty soon governments can't do things because they've given up those capabilities to the private sector. And private corporations don't necessarily maintain those capabilities."[5] That sounds like a pretty clear warning.

By the end of 2002, Allbaugh decided he had spent enough time diminishing our nation's capacity to respond to emergencies. Like other Bush cronies, Joe embarked on a new path, quickly figuring out ways to profit from his connections to the president and the war in Iraq. As his successor, he recommended his friend Michael Brown.

Michael Brown's qualifications to run a government agency to whom the American people literally trust their lives were even more questionable and scant than Allbaugh's. Brown ran for Congress in 1988 against Democrat Glenn English in Oklahoma and got less than 30 percent of the vote. After this embarrassment, Brown pledged to keep fighting, telling the *Daily Oklahoman*, "I have an excellent chance of prevailing. It's a Democratic state, but a very Republican district."[6] But as it turned out, Michael Brown had a higher calling than being a sacrificial lamb for the Republican Party. In 1989, Brown took a job as "Judges and Stewards Commissioner" for the International Arabian Horse Association.

This leads us to a couple of questions:

1. **What is the International Arabian Horse Association?**
    First, the organization no longer exists. In the wake of Mr. Brown's tenure, it merged with the Arabian Horse Registry of America. The now-defunct organization's ignoble mission was to set the standards by which wealthy, bored people could have their horses judged by other wealthy, bored people.

2. **What does the Judges and Stewards Commissioner do?**
    It turns out some of these wealthy, bored horse owners were cheating in a number of ways—including having expensive cosmetic surgery performed on their horses so they would perform better in competition. Our friend Michael Brown was brought in to investigate and crack down on these practices.

Of course, as he would at FEMA, Brown was coming in without any experience.[7]

3. How does being Judges and Stewards Commissioner of the International Arabian Horse Association qualify you to run FEMA?

It doesn't.

After appointing Brown, a glorified horse judge, and an inexperienced one at that, to run FEMA, Bush moved the agency out of the cabinet and into the Department of Homeland Security. Also in 2003, funding for FEMA's Hazard Mitigation Grant Program was cut in half—despite a FEMA report that noted about Louisiana, "flooding is a constant threat, and the state has an estimated 18,000 buildings that have been repeatedly damaged by flood waters—the highest number of any state."[8]

Helping New Orleans was clearly not a priority for the Bush administration. There were much more important things to get done—tax cuts for the rich, an endless war in Iraq, and jobs for cronies. In March 2004, FEMA's situation had grown critical. In fact, former director James Lee Witt told Congress he was "extremely concerned that the ability of our nation to prepare for and respond to disasters has been sharply eroded." Witt didn't pull any punches: "I hear from emergency managers, local and state leaders, and first responders nearly every day that the FEMA they knew and worked well with has now disappeared. In fact one state emergency manager told me, 'It is like a stake has been driven into the heart of emergency management.' "[9]

Instead of heeding the advice of one of the most successful emergency managers in history, Bush and Brown chose to ignore it, compounding the problem. On June 8, 2004, Walter Maestri, the emergency management chief for Jefferson Parish, Louisiana, told the *New Orleans Times-Picayune:* "It appears that the money has been moved in the president's budget to handle homeland security and the war in Iraq, and I suppose that's the price we pay. Nobody locally is happy that the levees can't be finished, and we are doing everything we can to make the case that this is a security issue for us."[10] George Bush made his choice, and the people of the Gulf coast were forced to pay for it.

Of course, these weren't the last cuts New Orleans would face from the Bush administration.

In 2005, an article in *New Orleans City Business* pointed out that "In fiscal year 2006, the New Orleans district of the U.S. Army Corps of Engineers is bracing for a record $71.2 million reduction in federal funding. It would be the largest single-year funding loss ever for the New Orleans district, Corps officials said. 'I've been here over 30 years and I've never seen this level of reduction,' said Al Naomi, project manager for the New Orleans district."[11]

The rest is history—although not quite as George Bush wrote it. In August, disaster struck. Katrina hit, the levees gave way, and the city flooded. Where was Bush? Sharing a birthday cake with John McCain, who was turning sixty-nine, as the streets and homes of the Lower Ninth Ward filled with water. Although that day Governor Blanco called Bush and asked for help, trying to explain the magnitude of the disaster, it wasn't until two days after that Bush even so much as flew over New Orleans.[12] (He didn't land, if you were wondering.)

Ironically, Republicans like to use Katrina as an example of the failure of government and an argument for privatization. Katrina is an example of how Bush's Republican-run government failed the American people. While no one can prevent hurricanes, the Bush administration at every turn exacerbated the aftermath of Katrina. New Orleans never had to flood, people never should have been trapped in the Convention Center, and the city should already be back to its best.

These failures of the Bush administration stemmed from the Bush-Norquist belief that government should be privatized and sold to the lowest bidder. Grover Norquist, the head of the Republican front-group Americans for Tax Reform, is known for having said he wanted to shrink government to the size where it could be "drowned in a bath tub." In New Orleans, he got his wish.

What truly struck me in the days following the storm was the callousness the Bush White House showed as the events unfolded. A Katrina timeline assembled by the impeccable Center for American Progress lays out the inaction by the White House, as the levees were breeched on Monday, August 29.[13]

7 AM CDT—*Katrina makes landfall as a category 3 hurricane.*[14]

7:30 AM CDT—*Bush Administration notified of the levee breach:* The administration finds out that a levee in New Orleans was breached. On this day, twenty-eight "government agencies, from local Louisiana parishes to the White House, [reported] that New Orleans levees" were breached.[15]

8 AM CDT—*Mayor Ray Nagin reports that water is flowing over. levee:* "I've gotten reports this morning that there is already water coming over some of the levee systems. In the lower ninth ward, we've had one of our pumping stations stop operating, so we will have significant flooding, it is just a matter of how much."[16]

11:13 AM CDT—*White House circulates internal memo about levee breach:* "Flooding is significant throughout the region and a levee in New Orleans has reportedly been breached sending 6–8 feet of water throughout the 9th ward area of the city."[17]

MORNING—*Brown warns Bush about the potential devastation of Katrina:* In a briefing, Brown warned Bush, "This is, to put it mildly, the big one, I think." He also voiced concerns that the government may not have the capacity to "respond to a catastrophe within a catastrophe" and that the Superdome was ill-equipped to be a refuge of last resort.[18]

MORNING—*Mayfield warns Bush about the topping of the levees:* In the same briefing, Max Mayfield, National Hurricane Center director, warns, "This is a category 5 hurricane, very similar to Hurricane Andrew in the maximum intensity, but there's a big big difference. This hurricane is much larger than Andrew ever was. I also want to make absolutely clear to everyone that the greatest potential for large loss of lives is still in the coastal areas from the storm surge. . . . I don't think anyone can tell you with any confidence right now whether the levees will be topped or not, but there's obviously a very very grave concern."[19]

MORNING—*Bush calls Secretary Chertoff to discuss immigration:* "I spoke to Mike Chertoff today—he's the head of the Department of Homeland Security. I knew people would want me to discuss this issue [immigration], so we got us an airplane on—a telephone on Air Force One, so I called him. I said, are you working with the governor? He said, you bet we are."[20]

MORNING—*Bush shares birthday cake photo-op with Sen. John McCain.*[21]

11 AM CDT—*Michael Brown finally requests that DHS dispatch 1,000 employees to region, gives them two days to arrive:* "Brown's memo to Chertoff described Katrina as 'this near catastrophic event' but otherwise lacked any urgent language. The memo politely ended, 'Thank you for your consideration in helping us to meet our responsibilities.' "[22]

11 AM CDT—*Bush visits Arizona resort to promote Medicare drug benefit:* "This new bill I signed says, if you're a senior and you like the way things are today, you're in good shape, don't change. But, by the way, there's a lot of different options for you. And we're here to talk about what that means to our seniors."[23]

LATE MORNING—*Levee breached:* "A large section of the vital 17th Street Canal levee, where it connects to the brand new 'hurricane proof' Old Hammond Highway bridge, gave way late Monday morning in Bucktown after Katrina's fiercest winds were well north."[24]

4:30 PM CDT—*Bush travels to California senior center to discuss Medicare drug benefit:* "We've got some folks up here who are concerned about their Social Security or Medicare. Joan Geist is with us. . . . I could tell—she was looking at me when I first walked in the room to meet her, she was wondering whether or not old George W. is going to take away her Social Security check."[25]

8 PM CDT—*Rumsfeld attends San Diego Padres baseball game:* Donald Rumsfeld "joined Padres President John Moores in the owner's box . . . at Petco Park."[26]

8 PM CDT—*Gov. Blanco again requests assistance from Bush:* "Mr. President, we need your help. We need everything you've got."[27]

LATE PM—*Bush goes to bed without acting on Blanco's requests.*

The next day, August 30, George Bush continued to ignore the situation in New Orleans, taking a break at 2 p.m. to play guitar with country singer Mark Wills before returning to Crawford for his final night of vacation. Only a day later did Bush survey the storm damage—from the comfort of Air Force One.

When the White House realized that a photo of the president looking out the window while New Orleaneans drowned might be ill-received, they quickly directed firefighters away from helping victims to participate in a photo-op with the president.

The Bush administration realized it was in trouble and moved to try to cast blame on local officials, putting politics before people in a very public, galling way. On Friday, September 2, just five days after the levees broke, "under the command of President Bush's two senior political advisers, the White House rolled out a plan . . . to contain the political damage from the administration's response to Hurricane Katrina."[28] Of course, just hours before was the first time George Bush had seen for himself the damage Katrina caused. Not in person, mind you.

Here's the telling passage from a *Newsweek* story entitled "How Bush Blew It":

The reality, say several aides who did not wish to be quoted because it might displease the president, did not really sink in until Thursday night. Some White House staffers were watching the evening news and thought the president needed to see the horrific reports coming out of New Orleans. Counselor Bartlett made up a DVD of the newscasts so Bush could see them in their entirety as he flew down to the Gulf Coast the next morning on Air Force One.[29]

The next day, George Bush started casting the blame on local officials directly. Here's what Bush passing the buck sounds like: "[T]he magnitude of responding to a crisis over a disaster area that is larger than the size of Great Britain has created tremendous problems that have strained state and local capabilities. The result is that many of our citizens simply are not getting the help they need."[30]

Officials in the Bush administration began dissembling and, well, outright lying, to try to save their own hides. *The Washington Post* reported, following the White House's lead, "As of Saturday, Blanco still had not declared a state of emergency, the senior Bush official said." They were forced to issue a correction hours later.[31]

Katrina proved what Democrats have known for a long time: Republican government does not work. You cannot underfund, disempower, and privatize government, and then expect it to be ready in times of need. What is scary is how Republicans have not learned the lesson of Katrina and are therefore doomed to repeat their mistakes. There are no signs of Republican atonement on the subject of Katrina, and no signs of abatement when it comes to the reckless and thoughtless abandonment of vital services to the private sector.

TRULY FAITH-BASED LIVING

There's a church in Ohio, near Dayton, called the Ginghamsburg United Methodist Church. They've got a $6 million annual budget, 120 staff, and a regular weekly attendance of 4,400 people, putting the self-identified evangelical haven that is Ginghamsburg firmly in the category of megachurch.

The thing that sets it apart, that distinguishes it and leads me to include it here, is the fact that this single church has sent forty-one teams of volunteers to Louisiana since Katrina hit— and they have six more scheduled to go in 2009.

The pastor of the Ginghamsburg United Methodist Church is one Reverend Mike Slaughter. He preaches in jeans, and he tells the members of the congregation, "you get no points for coming to church on Sunday."

Of course, the thing Slaughter says that stands out to me, and see if you can imagine having heard anything like this ever, is this: "If you don't want to serve, you won't fit in here. You'll eventually become uncomfortable."[32]

Members of the church pay to go on these mission trips. It's $3,000 to go to Thailand, and $2,000 to do work in the Czech Republic. People fund-raise and find sponsors so they can go, and they go multiple times in a year. One father-daughter set of congregants will go to New Orleans three times this year.

They don't exactly slack while back in Ohio, either. Each year at Christmas, members of the congregation turn to donations instead of holiday spending. In 2007 they gave more than $1 million. Their targeted efforts are no less impressive. Since 2005, the church has worked with the United Methodist Committee on Relief to raise more than $3 million for aid to Darfur.

The danger for these conservatives who insist on throwing the Bible at everyone is that people might actually pick it up and read the New Testament. Reverend Slaughter and the Ginghamsburg United Methodist Church are what happen when people read the Bible.

CHAPTER 5

The Democrats

You've heard my evidence for why the Republicans are going to keep losing. Now here's a few pages on why the Democrats are going to keep winning—and winning, and winning.

It's mostly math. You've heard quite a bit about polling, and after seeing what the Republicans did with polls, I can see how that might seem like a fuzzy, subjective thing, so let's walk through some hard numbers. Registration, turnout, and fund raising figures all dictate that the Democrats are building a strong advantage over Republicans. (You really can't underestimate the money. People lie about money, but money doesn't lie.) Following the election, the numbers point to a Democratic realignment. In other words, the Democrats are going to keep winning big for a long time.

The map's changing. Indiana, Virginia, and North Carolina all voted Democratic. In 2004, voters divided between the two parties equally at the polls, but in 2008, exit polls showed a 7-point advantage in party identification for Democrats. More to the point, Democrats had a 19-point advantage among voters aged eighteen to twenty-nine. Pause for a moment and read that again. That's right, a 19-point gap between the number of young people who called themselves Democrats and those who admitted to being Republicans. Before the Republicans try to dismiss it as a natural indiscretion of youth to vote for a Democrat a few times before they know better, you might want to remind them that in 2004 the Democrats had only a 2-point advantage in party identification.[1]

I'm not in the market to bore anyone by walking through each state's registration and turnout patterns. Instead, I'll offer some of the numbers that struck me back in June when I looked back through the primary.

- In South Dakota, Democratic voter registration increased by 5 percent from 2006
- More than half a million voters registered or switched registrations to vote in Democratic primaries in Pennsylvania, North Carolina, and Indiana alone
- Democratic primary turnout totaled 35.1 million
- Democratic primary turnout broke records in at least twenty-three states
- During the primary, turnout among 18–29-year-olds increased by 53 percent while 65+ turnout increased by 22 percent and 45+ turnout increased by 10 percent
- In South Dakota, Democratic turnout was slightly more than 50 percent—a new record
- 22 percent of the Democratic primary electorate nationwide had never before voted in a primary election
- In Virginia, 37 percent of voters had not voted in a primary before—a 12-point increase from 2004, when 25 percent were new voters.[2]

Democrats' gains were even clearer in the general election, when we could compare our side to Republicans. Democratic turnout was the highest in more than four decades everywhere but the South and the Southwest, where Democratic performance still hit a sixteen-year high. Democrats increased leads in the West, New England, and the mid-Atlantic states, and overtook the Republicans in the industrial Midwest and among farm states. Formerly unassailably solid Republican advantages in the South and mountain states shrank to unrecognizably slim margins.

For the specifics I'll turn it over to Curtis Gans of American University's Center for the Study of the American Electorate.

Democrats scored gains in every region of the nation. Their turnout in western states was 34.6 percent of eligibles, the highest since 1960; in the industrial Midwest (33.5 percent of eligibles), highest since 1964; in the farm Midwest (34.5), highest since 1964; in New England (42.9), highest ever; in mid-Atlantic states (34.4), highest since 1964; in mountain states (31.4), highest since 1964; in the Southwest, heavily skewed because of Texas's disproportionately sized population in the region (21.8), highest since 1992; and in the South (26.3), the highest since 1992, the last election before the 1994 anti-Clinton midterm which tipped southern congressional supremacy to the GOP.

The Democrats also extended their leads in regions where they already had strength and narrowed the gap where they have been behind. In the West, where Democrats had been ahead 30.5 percentage points to 24.8 for the Republicans in 2004, the 2008 margin was 34.6 to 20.4. In New England, where the pro-Democratic margin was 30.7 to 19, the 2008 margin was 42.9 to 15.2. In the mid-Atlantic states, where the Democratic lead had been 27.5 to 23.8, it widened in 2008 to 34.4 to 21.4. In the industrial Midwest, a 2004 GOP lead of 30.8 to 29.3 turned into a Democratic lead of 33.5 to 26.8. The GOP's 35.3 to 31.2 farm state advantage in 2004 turned into a Democratic advantage of 34.5 to 30.6.

In two regions which have been Republican strongholds, the Democrats substantially narrowed the gap. What had been a 28.8 to 20.1 percentage point advantage in the South narrowed to less than a percentage point (27.2 to 26.3). In the mountain states, what had been a 34.9 to 26.6 GOP advantage narrowed to 33.3 to 31.4.[3]

If you need some visuals to go along with the numbers, here they are: a packed stadium and an empty room. Obama literally filled stadiums while McCain couldn't even fill a few hundred chairs. Just look at June, when Obama had a crowd of 75,000 at a single event in Oregon. Meanwhile, when McCain gave his big Change speech in New Orleans, which an observer might recognize as an attempt to resuscitate his "maverick" image after cozying up to Bush, only 600 people showed up.[4]

The cash tide has also turned. And it's a huge turning point in American politics. Tiny donations, little checks from homemakers in Iowa and online donations from college students forgoing lattes have driven the biggest fund-raising numbers we've seen in U.S. political history. By June, as the Democratic primary was wrapping up, Obama had raised $265 million, three times as much as McCain, and had 1.5 million donors whose average contribution was less than $100.[5] Obama continued to outstrip McCain even with the McCain campaign collecting $28,500 in checks from oil company executives.[6] Ultimately, Obama raised $745 million to McCain's $320 million, including $84 million from the public financing system. When the American people's donations become as important as the corporate contributions, Democrats win. It's that simple.

CHAPTER 6

What Happened to Hillary

When I'm out and about around the country, people like to ask me who of the people I've met in politics I admire the most. In the past I've demurred and hedged and talked about President Clinton and some other remarkable people I've known. Today the obvious answer to that question is Hillary Clinton. However much I admired her at the beginning of the campaign as a person, that admiration has grown and grown for a thousand reasons—her grace under pressure, her ability to deal with disappointment, and so on.

Before I lay out my criticisms, and I have quite a few, I'm reminded of a comment by a very astute and acclaimed observer of the American political scene who spoke at my class at Tulane—he said, and I quote, "Hillary was the better candidate, but Obama had the better campaign." In the end, she couldn't make up for the lack of preparation, planning, and, well, not having a comprehensive strategy.

Four moments decided the fate of Hillary's campaign, in my mind.

If Barack Obama the human being was born on August 4, 1961 at 7:24 p.m., Barack Obama the presidential candidate was born at 12:50 a.m. on October 11, 2002. That is the day, the hour, and the minute that Senator Hillary Rodham Clinton voted to go to war in Iraq. That vote sank Kerry in 2004, and it sank Hillary in 2008. Hillary's vote for the war was the impetus for Obama to run against her. That vote was the single most important factor in her defeat.

Second would be the precise moment, whatever it may be, that it became clear that Hillary Clinton's chief strategist, Mark Penn, suffered fatal confusion on the subject of delegates. He denies it, but it's a poorly kept secret that Mr. Penn did not understand how California delegates are allocated in the Democratic primary. California, dear readers, is not a winner-take-all state. Mark Penn's strategy hinged on Hillary gaining all of California's 370 pledged delegates when she won the California primary rather than forfeiting 166 delegates to Obama and gaining only 204. That's a pretty spectacular error.

The third moment was 6:30 p.m. on December 15, 2007, the Saturday before the *Des Moines Register* endorsed Hillary Clinton. President Clinton, Terry McAuliffe, Justin Cooper, and myself, along with two Secret Service agents, were driving from a fundraiser in Palm Beach to Miami Beach. Terry McAuliffe matter-of-factly stated the campaign had only enough money left to buy television through New Hampshire and South Carolina—that's it. Iowa had already deteriorated for Hillary at that point. The former president and I had the same unprintable reaction. We called someone else familiar with campaign finances who confirmed what Terry McAuliffe said. Our panic was fully justified—they couldn't fund the field in eleven caucus states and the campaign had spent $10 million through Iowa already.

The fourth date was when my friend and then Democratic Congressional Caucus chairman Rahm Emanuel asked me to talk to a group of Democratic congress people about the political climate. It was Monday, April 14, 2008. Pennsylvania, Indiana, and North Carolina were just quickly approaching. A group of about fifteen gathered at the Monacle—a mix of African-American and white southern congressmen and women.

The conversation began on the congressional prospects for the fall. But naturally, the conversation quickly turned to the presidential contest. Several of the members asked what I thought of the battle ahead. Everyone knew I was for Hillary, but everyone knew I'd shoot straight with them, too.

I stated simply that I thought Hillary would have a better chance against John McCain in the general election for a variety of reasons. Almost all agreed. But these same superdelegates proceeded to say that they'd be for Obama for one reason or another in the end, mostly because they didn't want to split the party.

So there we were, Hillary with momentum after a few big wins, headed for a couple of wins in the near future, and they were going to be for Obama regardless.

I left dinner that night with a very pessimistic outlook for Hillary. Superdelegates and party leaders accepted that she was the stronger general election candidate, yet they were going to Obama. It put her campaign in a very difficult predicament. I suspect that she was hearing the same reactions on her phone calls and in her meetings with other superdelegates across the country.

As a general rule I hate campaign postmortems, but it's so Bushian to say we shouldn't look back, just forward, and not examine what happened or what could have been as opposed to what was. I think in many ways her achievement was utterly remarkable.

The most staggering achievement of the 2008 campaign, short of Obama's fund-raising, was that Hillary came back from eleven defeats. Quickly name another politician who's done that; or take all the time you want. You still won't be able to do it. She performed much better than Obama in the later stages of the campaign. She did win, by most accounts, probably twenty-four out of twenty-six debates. A total of 18 million Americans voted for her.

Aside from those five major points, I'd note just a few other structural and strategic issues with the Clinton campaign:

1. **It's the spending, stupid.**
   Complete lack of financial discipline, as evidenced by the fact that they spent $77 million before the Iowa caucus.[1]

2. **The "inevitability" strategy was just plain dumb.**
   It played into a preexisting perception among many voters, and literally all of the media, that she felt that she was entitled

to the nomination. To me that does not constitute an either appealing or uplifting message. Apparently no one else was enticed either.

I had hoped that early on they would make the election about something bigger than Hillary. I'm a one-trick pony on this topic, but energy—both the kinds we consume and the amounts we consume—would seem to me to be something that voters would have found refreshing and appealing. I can refer you to other parts of this book, numerous Democracy Corps memos, and past books that I've written, that have spoken about this issue extensively.

3. **You attract more reporters with honey than vinegar.**
The Clinton press strategy was flawed. They concluded that the press didn't like them and decided therefore they were going to aggressively push back as much as possible.

It has to be said, the Clinton campaign was right. The press didn't, and still doesn't, like Hillary. I know a lot of people in the press, and I have never heard anyone try to claim that the press was not vehemently anti-Hillary in general. I have certainly heard journalists defend their own coverage, but it is an acknowledged fact that the press enthusiastically favored Senator Barack Obama.

But the campaign made a bad situation awful instead of riding it out or making it, well, less bad. I will defend their general observation that the press hated them and liked Obama, but I can't defend their strategy of engaging in a war with the press.

They could have made the situation better. They should have engaged the press, been more available, had a better attitude toward them, and dealt with them on an up-and-up basis. Instead, their attitude was, you need us more than we need you.

When Clinton fell behind, this bit those in the campaign in the ass. It's a chicken-and-egg thing, but they could never stop showing their contempt for the press, and the press could never stop showing their contempt for Senator Clinton. I don't think anyone in the press wants to revisit the primary, because everyone knows what the truth is. The truth is, they didn't like her and she didn't like them.

4. There was no one in charge.

I wasn't involved in the campaign. I didn't have a position. I wasn't paid by it. I was a supporter, a contributor, and an admirer only. But until later in the campaign, no one had clear authority. It was a campaign where it was easier to get something stopped than get something done. They could have had better established lines of authority.

5. They didn't have a Plan B.

Plan A was that she would win Iowa and New Hampshire and everything would be fine. They didn't have a Plan B. They came up with one pretty fast, and actually finished a lot better than Obama did; but the Clinton campaign's decision not even to try in some caucus states was indefensible.

While I'm talking about Hillary, I have to address a question her critics ask me unfailingly: If her campaign was so badly run, how could you think she'd be a better president? The only answer is: Bush had a well-run campaign. The kind of campaign you run doesn't have much to do with the type of president you'd be.

A Word About Bill Clinton

I have gladly and proudly defended President Clinton. When he did something wrong, my simply stated, oft-repeated answer was that he was a good man who did a bad thing.

About the primary and the summer to follow I can write that he's a good man who didn't do a bad thing. The charges being played out in the media during the primary were idiotic. I have no idea what the problem with Clinton was in the primary. Best I can tell, the only sin he committed was that of vigorously and enthusiastically supporting his wife. Granted, from time to time, his vigor and enthusiasm detracted from her getting her message out, but that's a matter for the Clintons to settle.

And while we're on Bill Clinton, let me state that his legacy is clear. Under the Clinton administration, we experienced unprecedented levels of prosperity. America was a nation respected around the world. His legacy is the highest end-of-office rating of any president since World War II, when Gallup started tracking those numbers.

I hardly believe that a vigorous defense of his wife is going to affect that legacy very much.

CHAPTER 7

A Brief History of Republican Failures: The e-Edition

After Senator John McCain admitted to being computer-"illiterate," the McCain campaign's best efforts at damage control amounted to assuring the American people that "Senator McCain is aware of the internet."[1] As part of his continuing effort to recover from his admission, McCain tried again, this time saying, "I do understand the importance of the computer. I understand the importance of the blogs."[2]

Democrats aren't just beating Republicans online—we're spanking them, as Carville would say. The competition isn't even close. Obama left McCain in the dust last year, in the process establishing online networks and lists that will ensure continued Democratic success in organizing and fund-raising online.

Republicans will try to rebut most of the arguments and evidence presented in this book. Even the ones that are *res judicata*, or settled. To refute Carville's points on energy, they'll brandish "experts" bankrolled by ExxonMobil to say there's no such thing as climate change. For the chapter on the economy, they'll produce a few questionable authorities of dubious academic accomplishment to defend supply-side insanity. Along the way they'll toss in a few personal attacks—Carville is a party hack, a sycophant, a mere mouthpiece twisting the facts.

But not even the Republicans can argue with this chapter—in

fact, throughout it, we'll be relying on top Republican operatives to help us make the case. Put simply, Democrats are light-years ahead online. Our candidates' Web sites get more visits. We have larger email lists. Our blogs are more popular. Finally, we have exponentially greater success raising funds online.

Even the top online consultants in the Republican Party admit how far behind conservatives are.

Take David All, a former Republican staffer and one of their top online guys. He admitted that "the problem is no longer simply a failure to communicate effectively in a modern world, but Republican candidates are now failing to match, or even come close to, Democrats in online contributions."[3]

All isn't alone. Michael Turk, the former eCampaign Director for the Republican National Committee, put it more bluntly when he said, "We're losing the Web right now."[4]

Republicans lie, but numbers don't. By every metric, conservatives are losing online. Let's start with the easiest numbers, online fund-raising. Ironically, the first big success in the political online fund-raising world was not Howard Dean's campaign—it was John McCain's in 2000.

McCain might not know how to use a computer, but in the two days following his win in New Hampshire in 2000, his Web site raked in more than $1 million in donations.[5] That's chump change by today's standards, but in 2000 it was an impressive haul—one that would not be matched until 2004.

McCain's success was not an accident. He'd taken his cue from former Minnesota governor Jesse Ventura, who raised $70,000 online in 1998. Believing the Internet would be an important part of the 2000 campaign, "McCain sent advisors to Minnesota last year to borrow from the Internet playbook of Gov. Jesse Ventura. . . . The plans appear to have paid off."[6]

Although McCain and Ventura's early success made conservatives hopeful they could dominate the medium, they quickly fell behind. Since 2000, Republicans have been unable to compete with Democrats online.

In 2004, Howard Dean used online activists to propel him from being the obscure governor of a small state to front-runner for the Democratic nomination. Dean didn't make it to the White House, or even to the Democratic nomination, but his success caused other Democrats to stand up and take notice.

As Dean himself noted, much of the campaign's early success was an accident: "We fell into this by accident," he admitted. "I wish I could tell you we were smart enough to figure this out. But the community taught us. They seized the initiative through Meetup. They built our organization for us before we had an organization."[7]

With a nod to Carville, who, as his wife, Mary Matalin, points out, thought the Internet was a special highway as recently as a few years ago, here's a quick history of Meetup and the Dean campaign for those who don't know it:

Meetup is a Web tool for forming social groups. In early 2003, Dean himself was lured to an early New York City Meetup where he found more than 300 enthusiastic supporters waiting to greet him. Meetup quickly became the engine of Dean's Internet campaign. Back then, the leading group on the site was a club for witches. Zephyr Teachout, Dean's director of Internet outreach, describes sitting across from campaign manager Joe Trippi in the early weeks and hitting refresh again and again on her Web browser. "I was obsessed with beating Witches," she says. "Witches had 15,000 members, and we had 3,000. I wanted first place."[8]

Dean was the first candidate to effectively use mass movement organizing online to fuel his campaign. Some of this was Meetup, but much of it took place through his email list. Dean's email list reached more than 600,000 people at its peak and was the primary force behind the $25 million he raised online.

Democrats have achieved this type of edge before, only to let it slip away. It was the Democratic Party that pioneered the use of direct-mail fund-raising, only to see Republicans use the technique more effectively for the next twenty years.

To channel Carville for a moment, let's take a quick trip to the archives:

In 1970, George McGovern, the way-long-shot antiwar candidate, began to experiment with the novel political fund-raising technique of direct mail to finance his unlikely primary race.

This political marketing strategy, according to an article that appeared in September 1972, was the brainchild of Morris Dees, who would become among the most prominent southern liberal activists, but who was then the head of a publishing company that sold special-interest books through the mail.

The idea—born not so much from marketing brilliance as from a lack of fund-raising alternatives—was to use the mail to solicit people who had already identified themselves as likely McGovern partisans. It was the method, not the goal, that was new—after all, politicians are always looking for help from their core supporters.

But the method introduced a heightened efficiency into the process. Almost all of the mail sent by the McGovern team went to three groups. You got a solicitation if you subscribed to liberal magazines: *The New Republic, The New York Review of Books, Ramparts,* or *Bulletin of the Atomic Scientists,* for instance. If your name appeared on lists maintained by organizations like Americans for Democratic Action or the ACLU or Zero Population Growth, you got a letter. Or if your name and address had been among the hundreds of thousands collected over the years of the antiwar movement (perhaps you had contributed to the campaign to support the end-the-war McGovern-Hatfield amendment), you got a sincere, well-crafted, multipage pitch from the McGovern marketers.[9]

Republicans took note of McGovern's success, and they quickly threw themselves into building their own direct-mail lists. Democrats, perhaps burned by the outcome of the general election, let their advantage slip away. There would have been incredible opportunities to build direct-mail lists during the Watergate era, which would be the height of dissatisfaction with Republican governance until Bush. But we let Watergate pass by, instead opting to focus on large donors and soft money.

Democrats would not repeat the same mistakes in the online world. While the Republican Party dismissed McCain's success in 2000, Democrats took their cue from Howard Dean and began to build on his successes. In December 2003, while he was still a long shot for the nomination, John Kerry spent time building a strong Internet operation.

Kerry's online turnaround was dramatic. While raising only a little more than $1 million online in all of 2003, by August 2004 he had raised more than $80 million. The *New York Times* reported, somewhat wonderingly, that "The Internet helped Mr. Kerry cut President Bush's financial lead substantially. Mr. Bush raised about $273 million, while Mr. Kerry raised about $249 million. The amount Mr. Kerry raised online virtually ensures that few presidential and Congressional campaigns will develop in the future without the Internet in mind."[10]

Add to that $80 million the tens of millions of dollars the Kerry campaign raised online after the convention to help fund the Democratic Party, and you can see the difference the online world made in 2004.

By comparison, Bush was able to raise only $14 million through the Internet, even after three years unchallenged as the leader of the Republican Party and despite incredible popularity among the Republican base.[11] Quick math says that Bush's $14 million goes into Kerry's $80 million almost 6 times.

After that miserable November, John Kerry and Howard Dean could have packed it in and called it a day. Instead, both decided to use their online infrastructure to help the party as a whole. Howard Dean turned Dean for America into Democracy for America, using his email list and network of local chapters to help candidates around the country. Meanwhile, Kerry took his email list and fund-raised for Democrats running for the House and Senate. In the 2006 cycle, Kerry ended up raising millions for other Democrats—an impressive feat. Today, the applications for Hillary's and Obama's lists are tremendous.

In 2008, Democratic dominance of online fund-raising has continued. From January to March 2007—yes, 2007—Clinton, Obama, and John Edwards raised more than $14 million online. Compare that to the anemic $6 million scraped together by McCain, Mitt Romney, and Rudolph Giuliani.[12] As of June 2008, Barack Obama had already raised more online than John McCain had for his entire campaign.

Remember that part about how numbers don't lie? Numbers may not lie, but Republicans still try to lie about numbers. When the Romney campaign filed its first-quarter report to the Federal Elections Commission in 2007, it claimed Romney had raised $7.2 million online—proof of deep, widespread support. That would have put Romney $300,000 ahead of Obama and $3 million stronger than Hillary online. Problem was, $7.2 million would be nearly a third of his total fund-raising.[13]

Romney was just shuffling large donors to the Web, defying the purpose of Internet fund-raising as a way to gather new, small-dollar, and grassroots donations. As far as the numbers go, the important one here is the dollars-to-donors ratio. A fellow Republican, Michael Turk, the eCampaign Director for Bush-Cheney 04 and the Republican National Committee, notes, "Romney reports about 20,000 donors who gave less than $200 and another 12,000 who gave more than $200 . . . there's no way Romney's online numbers add up to more than $7 million unless his team directed many of his maxed-out contributors—people giving $2,300 each—to give via credit card on his website."[14]

It's one thing in politics to exaggerate your success. It's another to outright lie, try to make yourself something you are not, then get caught. If Republicans had any capacity for shame, the Romney camp would have to be somewhat embarrassed.

Online fund-raising is the easiest metric for candidates; but what's even more impressive than Democrats' online fund-raising is the movement we've been able to build up online. Barack Obama communicated with more than 13 million Americans through his email list. He asked them to take real action to deliver his message—knock on doors, make phone calls, talk to their friends. His email list gave the campaign an opportunity to have the equivalent of a daily conference call with all of his most active supporters every day.

The campaign also used my.barackobama.com as a platform for supporters to gather to take action. The campaign even used the Internet to check in on how far-flung field staff were performing.

While covering the Personal Democracy Forum conference in New York, *Politico*'s Ben Smith wrote, "One of the interesting revelations is that they've been using online feedback to keep tabs on their field staff, in the form of a questionnaire sent to supporters in primary states who interacted with Obama's staff or volunteers. [Obama's new media director Joe] Rospars said the campaign had produced a long report based on the 'hundreds of thousands of responses.' 'We know who the staff were in different congressional districts, and what the performance was,' he said, citing a level of staff accountability familiar from elements of the service industry but utterly unknown to politics."[15]

The fact that an entire online movement numbering in the tens of millions exists is a testament to Barack Obama and the campaign he chose to run. One that is powered not only with Internet dollars, but with real grassroots support organized online.

It's not only our candidates who have been more impressive online. What really puts Democrats over the top is activism from our grassroots supporters. Nothing exemplifies this more than ActBlue. The mission statement on the ActBlue Web site reads: "ActBlue is a political committee that enables anyone—individuals, local groups, and national organizations—to fundraise online for the Democratic candidates of their choice."[16] ActBlue has raised more than $88 million for Democrats since 2004. Most Democratic candidates have received contributions through ActBlue. In 2006, Senator Jim Webb of Virginia raised almost $850,000 on ActBlue and Senator Jon Tester of Montana raised close to $350,000. The right wing tried to imitate the success of ActBlue with RightRoots. com. So far their efforts don't even come close, in dollars raised, candidates supported, or any other metric that means anything. In February, Right Roots attempted to plan a big fund-raising campaign called "F7 2008: One Day to Stop Hillary and F7 2008: One Day to Stop Obama." According to the events description, "One Day to Stop Hillary (and Obama) is a grassroots campaign by Right Roots to mobilize thousands of Republican donors to contribute to our party's nominee on Thursday, February 7, 2008. This critical date falls two days after the 'Super Duper Tuesday' primary on February 5th, the soonest (and still most likely) date that the presumptive nominee will be known."[17]

How did they do? According to a graphic on their site, they raised $2,646 from thirty-two donors. To use a favorite printable expression of James's, that's pathetic.

The Blogosphere

The progressive blogosphere puts its conservative counterpart, or lack thereof, to shame. From the *Huffington Post* to *Daily Kos* to *Open Left* to Americablog, we've got bigger readership and a greater ability to direct audiences to action. While not a perfect metric, a quick look at blog traffic on BlogAd.com reveals the top ten liberal blogs combined have 19,414,394 impressions per week, while the top ten conservative blogs lag far behind with 4,710,244 impressions per week.[18]

It is not just size or traffic that matters. While conservative blogs claim the scalp of Dan Rather, Josh Marshall of *Talking Points Memo* can take credit for having pursued the U.S. Attorney scandal until the media finally paid attention.

Name That Idiot

Here are the rules for a fun and simple drinking game for you and your progressive friends. Get yourselves some alcohol and get ready for a good time. The first person up names a Republican idiot and gives a detail about his or her particular brand of corruption and incompetence. Participants to follow have to come up with a new name and corresponding information or offer a new detail on a previously mentioned idiot. If you can't come up with something, drink. (It goes without saying that if you get something wrong, you also have to drink.)

To look at the other accomplishments of the progressive blogosphere, we need only to turn to Harry Reid and his speech to the YearlyKos Convention in 2006:

As a former boxer, I know a fighter—and a winner—when I see one, and as Senate Democratic Leader, I'm glad there are so many of you fighting on our side. Whether it's spreading the truth or fighting for what's right, you have made a tremendous difference for our country and the Democratic Party. It was you who was quick to stand against the Swift Boat Smear of John Kerry. It was you who defended Valerie Plame and Joe Wilson against Scooter Libby, Dick Cheney and Karl Rove. It was you who helped Democrats win key victories in Social Security and the Nuclear Option. And it is you—today—who are making sure the truth is heard.19

The blogosphere also played an active role in Ned Lamont's primary win in Connecticut and in the Web-fueled elections of both Senator Jim Webb and Senator Jon Tester.

The explanation for Democrats' success online is simple. Successful efforts online, from MoveOn.org to Dean to Obama, involve open communication and opportunities for participation. Interaction builds and sustains communities. It's no surprise that Democrats excel at building movements and enthusiasm in this democratic medium.

When it comes to the Internet, there are three core questions. First, "How much money can you raise?" Then, "How many people can you get signed up?" And, finally, "How many voters can you get to the polls?" Democrats beat Republicans on all three metrics—indisputably, irrefutably, and dramatically, in fact—and Republicans have little hope of catching up in time to do anything about the emerging Democratic majority.

CHAPTER 8

Res Judicata:
We Argue About Things That Aren't Arguable

You can argue about a lot of things. We can debate abortion, capital punishment, religion in schools, snowmobiles in National Parks, all sorts of things. Other things are simply inarguable. If a person walks up to you and says, "I think being gay is a choice," that's not grounds for an argument—that's the moment for you to say, "You need to check yourself into a mental hospital."

The point of this chapter is to point out that we've got to stop arguing that which has already been decided. There's a Latin term you learn in law school, *res judicata*. It's been adjudicated. It's been decided.

The earth is warming. Evolution occurred. The planet is not 5,000 years old. Who begat whom who begat whom is not history, and it isn't geology. Teaching sex education in schools is necessary—and abstinence-only education doesn't work. And, by the way, the Republicans stole Florida in 2000.

Here's a list of topics on which there is no argument:

- Global warming
- Evolution
- Age of the earth
- Grand Canyon
- Abstinence-based education

- HPV vaccine
- That being gay is a choice
- Florida

What are we arguing about?

Global Warming Is Happening, and It's Caused by Humans. Period.

THE RIGHT

"Today, even saying there is scientific disagreement over global warming is itself controversial. But anyone who pays even cursory attention to the issue understands that scientists vigorously disagree over whether human activities are responsible for global warming, or whether those activities will precipitate natural disasters."[1]

WHY WE'RE RIGHT/THE SCIENCE

Global warming is established fact, and it is caused by human activity, according to the UN Intergovernmental Panel on Climate Change, the National Academy of Sciences, the American Meteorological Society, and the American Geophysical Union.[2]

The dangerous effects of global warming are staring us right in the face and are clear to anyone who isn't intentionally putting blinders on. In the summer of 2009—for the first time in recorded history—the North Pole could have no sea ice.[3] Sea levels are rising across the globe.[4] Glaciers are retreating across the globe.[5] We are seeing more and more extreme and altered weather patterns.[6]

These changes to our climate are not just an academic discussion; they have direct and dangerous impacts on our economy. According to the UN Intergovernmental Panel on Climate Change, dangers include disruption to agriculture, problems in insurance and investment markets, infrastructure degradation, water scarcity, and increasing health problems.[7]

I just can't let this go, and no one should, so let me add here—global warming is a huge security threat. For all that President Bush and the Republicans want to claim that they take the strong stand on national security, global warming may be the greatest threat Americans will face in the coming years.[8] (For more on this, turn to Chapter 14 on The Real Deal.)

What do the Republicans do in the face of overwhelming scientific evidence? Imagine a two-year-old's temper tantrum. I'm talking about the really bad kind, when a child summons up every bit of righteous indignation he can, sticks his fingers in his ears, and screams at the top of his lungs so he can't hear you. That pretty much sums up the Republicans' attitude.

The Senate Republicans' point person on the environment is Senator James Inhofe, who claims that climate change is the "greatest hoax ever perpetrated on the American people." He's the one who warns that "Much of the debate over global warming is predicated on fear, rather than science."[9]

The Bush administration has gone to great lengths to shut out all discussion of global warming. For one, they've censored the Environmental Protection Agency. In 2003, the EPA tried to publish a draft report on the environment, exactly the sort of activity one would imagine an agency on the environment was created to undertake. The Bush administration essentially gutted the section on global warming, whittling it down to a few feeble paragraphs.

A damning *Washington Monthly* article investigated the Bush response to global warming and reported that "curious reporters asking the White House about climate change are sent to a small, and quickly diminishing, group of scientists who still doubt the causes of global warming."[10] The Bush administration is set on trying to create its own reality when it comes to global warming. After the Intergovernmental Panel on Climate Change published a report on climate change—and please bear in mind this was the work of 2,500 leading scientists—the Bush administration ordered its own scientists to create a follow-up. In the words of Nicholas

Thompson, it was "like asking a district court to review a Supreme Court decision."

To return to my earlier, appropriate analogy of the Bush administration reacting to science like a two-year-old told no, it would appear that the adult equivalent of plugging your ears with your fingers is to ignore emails. The Bush administration's latest trick to ignore the EPA was simply to stop opening emails from them.[11]

While the Republicans were refusing to accept basic scientific facts, the Democrats were trying to pass legislation that will combat global warming and promote energy independence, but had to pull the bill because Republicans would not support it.[12] Until the Republicans accept that global warming is not a topic for debate, we'll have to rely on outside groups—and leaders like Al Gore—to take action on climate change.

Evolution Occurred

On evolution, what is there to say? There is possibly no better illustration of just how ridiculous the Republican Party has become than their insistence on government endorsement of creationism. If there's ever been a time to use the word "incontrovertible," it's when we're talking about evolution. Arguing evolution is like denying gravity. Creationist propaganda has no place in our schools. Of course, that's a truth based on science and law—two subjects Republicans have little regard for.

THE RIGHT

"Intelligent design postulates that humans originated due to the intentional arrangement of bio-matter—including the human genetic code—by the action of intelligence."[13]

THE RIGHT, TAKE 2

Intelligent design "begins with the observation that intelligent agents produce complex and specified information (CSI).... One easily testable form of CSI is irreducible complexity, which can be discovered by experimentally reverse-engineering biological structures to see if they require all of their parts to function. When [intelligent design] researchers find irreducible complexity in biology, they conclude that such structures were designed." [14]

Basically, because they don't understand evolution, and they can't replicate it, these intelligent design "scientists" have decided it can't have taken place.

WHY WE'RE RIGHT/THE SCIENCE

"In science, a theory is a rigorously tested statement of general principles that explains observable and recorded aspects of the world. A scientific theory therefore describes a higher level of understanding that ties 'facts' together. A scientific theory stands until proven wrong—it is never proven correct. The Darwinian theory of evolution has withstood the test of time and thousands of scientific experiments; nothing has disproved it since Darwin first proposed it more than 150 years ago. Indeed, many scientific advances, in a range of scientific disciplines including physics, geology, chemistry, and molecular biology, have supported, refined, and expanded evolutionary theory far beyond anything Darwin could have imagined." [15]

The issue of evolution in school curricula truly is *res judicata*. Not to bore you, dear reader, but let's review the body of legal precedent that supports the science.

We all know about the "monkey" trial—the Scopes trial in Tennessee in 1925. That was the first major legal test of evolution in schools, but it wasn't until forty years later that the U.S. Supreme Court ruled on evolution.

In 1968, the Supreme Court took on the issue of evolution in *Epperson* v. *Arkansas*. The Court ruled that evolution is science and creationism is religion. Ergo, evolution can be taught in schools and creationism cannot. It's a simple First Amendment issue. Twenty years after that, the Supreme Court found itself faced with another evolution issue, this time coming from Louisiana—*Edwards* v. *Aguilar*. In 1987, the Court ruled against the Louisiana law requiring schools to teach both evolution and creationism together.[16]

Despite 150 years of science and 80 years of law, there's a whole active movement among conservatives to push intelligent design again. A Gallup Poll found that 60 percent of Republicans believe that man was created by God 10,000 years ago, as is.[17] That means six of ten Republicans don't believe in evolution. The Republicans have bought into intelligent design and they are fighting to make it a policy issue.

Take, for example, the 2008 pseudo-documentary *Expelled: No Intelligence Allowed*, which was of enough note and profile that the *New York Times* took aim at it—and gave it a deservingly scathing review.

The so-called documentary on the "debate" over evolution and creationism was unapologetic propaganda masquerading as science. The filmmakers were "linking evolution theory to fascism (as well as abortion, euthanasia and eugenics), shamelessly invoking the Holocaust with black-and-white film of Nazi gas chambers and mass graves." The review read: "Positing the theory of intelligent design as a valid scientific hypothesis, the film frames the refusal of 'big science' to agree as nothing less than an assault on free speech."[18] Meanwhile, I consider the proposal to teach intelligent design in schools nothing short of an attack on the U.S. Constitution, the integrity of our public schools, and Americans' intelligence.

Just look at what Republican elected officials have to say.

George W. Bush is of the mind that students should learn about both evolution and intelligent design. That's like saying it should be up to individual school boards to decide when the country was founded. According to Bush, "Both sides ought to be properly taught . . . so people can understand what the debate is about. . . . Part of education is to expose people to different schools of thought. . . . You're asking me whether or not people ought to be exposed to different ideas, and the answer is yes."[19]

The fact that Bush was for teaching intelligent design should be enough for other Republicans to know to be against it, but they're all still for it, too.

Think back to the dishearteningly dissembling discussion of evolution that transpired at the June 2007 Republican presidential debate in New Hampshire. We can look to the statement of Governor Mike Huckabee of Arkansas, who actually had a shot at the Republican nomination, frighteningly enough. "To me it's pretty simple. A person either believes God created this process or it was an accident, and that it all happened just all on its own . . . but you know if anybody wants to believe that they are the descendants of a primate, they are certainly welcome to do it, I don't know how far they will march that back."[20]

At that same debate John McCain, who was then touting himself as a moderate, got more than a touch closer to the crazy far right himself. McCain said that he thought that whether schools teach intelligent design should be "up to the school districts" and that "every American should be exposed to all theories." McCain even went so far as to say he admired Huckabee's views on the topic. His final statement on the matter was that he believes "all of our children in school can be taught different views on different issues."[21] The modern Republican Party doesn't seem to understand the difference between fact and opinion.

There's always Ron Paul. I admit the possibility that I am throwing this in for my own amusement, but here goes: "I think it's a theory, *theory* of evolution, and I don't accept it . . . I just don't think we're at the point where anybody has absolute proof on either side."[22]

And on down the ranks. Senator Sam Brownback said it would be "helpful" to talk about intelligent design "in a bit more detail and with the seriousness it demands."[23] The seriousness it demands? The amount of seriousness intelligent design deserves is somewhat less than the amount of seriousness I devote to the idea of becoming a monk.

Republicans even try to blame the teaching of evolution for problems in the world. After the shootings at Columbine High

School in California, Representative Tom DeLay, former Republican majority leader, blamed youth violence on "the teaching of evolution" along with, of course, "working parents who put their kids into daycare . . . and working mothers who take birth control."[24] That's an offensive new low, even for DeLay.

The Democratic answer is simple. Obama nailed it. When asked about teaching evolution in schools, he said: "I believe there's a difference between science and faith. That doesn't make faith any less important than science. It just means they're two different things. And I think it's a mistake to try to cloud the teaching of science with theories that frankly don't hold up to scientific inquiry."[25]

Senator Clinton has also been consistently effective in her responses, saying reasonably and respectfully, "I believe that our founders had faith in reason and they also had faith in God, and one of our gifts from God is the ability to reason."[26]

Although former Governor Howard Dean and I have some points of disagreement, I find myself wholly behind him when it comes to his take on evolution. Dean got it right on *Face the Nation*: "Science is science. There's no factual evidence for intelligent design. There's an enormous amount of factual evidence for evolution. Those are the facts. If you don't like the facts, then you can fight against them. The Catholic Church fought against Galileo for a great many, many centuries."[27]

Representative Rush Holt of New Jersey is actually a physicist. (How a physicist got to the House is beyond me, so don't ask.) He got predictably worked up over the idea of teaching intelligent design in school, and he offered a rather clear scientific indictment of intelligent design:

> Sure, evolution is a theory, just as gravitation is a theory. The mechanisms of evolution are indeed up for debate, just as the details of gravitation and its mathematical relationship with other forces of nature are up for debate. Some people once believed that we are held on the ground by invisible angels above

us beating their wings and pushing us against the earth. If angels always adjusted their beating wings to exert force that diminished as the square of the distance between attracting bodies, it would be just like our idea of gravitation. The existence of those angels, undetected by any measurements, would not be the subject of science. Such an idea of gravity is "not even wrong." It is beyond the realm of science. So, too, is intelligent design.[28]

So there you have it, the so-called debate over evolution boils down to the Republicans' invisible-angel theory of gravity against the Democrats' 150 years of science and the U.S. Constitution position.

Of course the statement on evolution I may agree with most closely is that of former Senator Mike Gravel of Alaska (for the first and only time). When someone asked Gravel if he thought creationism and intelligent design should be taught in schools, he responded: "Oh God, no. Oh, Jesus. We thought we had made a big advance with the Scopes monkey trial. . . . My God, evolution is a fact, and if these people are disturbed by being the descendants of monkeys and fishes, they've got a mental problem. We can't afford the psychiatric bill for them. That ends the story as far as I'm concerned."[29]

The Earth Is Not Thousands of Years Old; It's Billions of Years Old

THE RIGHT

"If you have ever wondered how old the earth and our universe is, just read the Bible. Begin at Genesis 1:1 and see how God created the heaven and the earth. Read all of Genesis chapter 1 and chapter 2 and understand that God created this entire present world in just six literal 24-hour days. . . . It is very clear . . .

that the Bible proves the age of our universe to be approximately 6,000 years old."[30]

THE RIGHT, TAKE 2

"The Bible provides a complete genealogy from Adam to Jesus. You can go through the genealogies and add up the years. You'll get a total that is just over 4,000 years. Add the 2,000 years since the time of Jesus and you get just over 6,000 years since God created everything. Is there anything wrong with figuring out the age of the earth this way? No. There is nothing to indicate the genealogies are incomplete. There is nothing to indicate God left anything out. There is nothing in the Bible that indicates in any way that the world is older than 6,000 years old."[31]

WHY WE'RE RIGHT/THE SCIENCE

"Science unequivocally dates the earth's age at 4.5 billion years. . . . Even the intelligent design movement, which argues that evolution alone cannot explain life's complexity, does not challenge the long history of the earth."[32]

Here's another fact for you: only 5 percent of scientists, and only 1 percent of earth and life scientists, believe in the "Young Earth" theory.[34] I'm a big proponent of the Bible, but I don't use it as a

---

Maher: But, why shouldn't it be part of a political discussion? If someone believes that the earth is 6,000 years old when every scientist in the world tells us it's billions of years old, why shouldn't I take that into account when I'm assessing the rationality of someone I'm going to put into the highest office in the land? [applause, cheers]

Huckabee: Well, I think the point, though, Bill, is that we really don't know. And that's my whole point.[33]

textbook for biology or geology any more than I'd try to explain the gospels with physics.

There are few things crazier than arguing about the age of the earth. The only time I ever want to hear about "Young Earth" theories is when we're pointing out that anyone who says the earth is "young" is unfit to be elected to office by reason of insanity.

God Didn't Create the Grand Canyon 4,500 Years Ago

I don't care if you want to believe the Grand Canyon is a few thousand years old, but keep your beliefs out of government. This isn't arguable. Bush was guilty of trying to enforce ideology at the expense of science through government. As Chris Mooney, author of a particularly solid book, *The Republican War on Science*, put it in 2005, "Dear President Bush: Americans don't want you to be a geologist. We only want you to talk to geologists when it becomes necessary for your job."[35]

THE RIGHT

"Bible-believing Christians interpret the canyon as a spillway from Noah's Flood. . . . The Bible says that a flood covered the whole earth (see Genesis 7:18–20). This means we should find places where the water drained. The Grand Canyon is one of those places. It is a washed-out spillway and provides great evidence for Noah's Flood."[36]

WHY WE'RE RIGHT/THE SCIENCE

"The Grand Canyon was formed 17 million years ago over a very, very long stretch of time. Several small streams eroded land away and joined together as the Colorado river, which carved out the Grand Canyon. Science proves it with uranium-lead dating and calcite deposits and every other test you can think of."[37]

The Republicans have given themselves over entirely to these Christian right crazies. These nut jobs hang out together. They create literature and pamphlets and even theme parks. My new favorite tourist destination has to be Dinosaur Adventure Land in Pensacola, Florida, where visitors come to hear about how man and dinosaurs co-existed.[38]

The Dinosaur Adventure Land Web site promises "a theme park and science museum that gives God the glory for His creation. It has rides and fun-filled events and activities, each involving a physical challenge, a science lesson, and a biblical truth." To be clear, the site offers that it is less an amusement park than "an amazement park. Come and stand amazed at the truths of the Creator and Savior of the world, Jesus Christ."[39] The truth they're teaching the young children who come to their Dinosaur Adventure Land being that humans and dinosaurs lived side by side in some kind of biblical Jurassic Park.

Unfortunately, they aren't limiting their craziness to their delusional dinosaur-themed parks. They're taking over National Parks.

About 4 million people visit the Grand Canyon National Park yearly. However many thousands of them who go into the park stores can buy right-wing propaganda along with bumper stickers and keychains, thanks to the National Parks Service. The Grand Canyon bookstores now sell a particularly ludicrous book—and I use the term "book" loosely—by the title *Grand Canyon, a Different View*. The author, one Mr. Tom Vail, is a Christian right crazy who gives guided creationist tours of the Grand Canyon.[40]

So from 2003 to 2008 the Grand Canyon bookstore has sold a book by a creationist that spells out how the Grand Canyon was created 4,500 years ago in Noah's Flood. (I say "to 2008" because I have yet to have the opportunity to attempt to call and verify whether the bookstore has continued to stock this work.) By the way, in 2003, twenty-two titles were rejected by Grand Canyon officials. Only the creationist manifesto made it through the no-doubt rigorous selection process.[41] Nothing subtle about that.

Wilfred Elders, professor of geology emeritus at the University of California Riverside, wrote that the book was " 'Exhibit A' of a new, slick strategy by biblical literalists to proselytize using a beautifully illustrated, multi-authored book about a spectacular and world-famous geological feature. . . . Allowing the sale of this book within the National Park was unfortunate. In the minds of some buyers, this could imply NPS approval of young-earth creationists and their religious proselytizing."[42]

A disgruntled park geologist was, shall we say, less kind. He said it would be like Yellowstone National Park offering *Geysers of Old Faithful: Nostrils of Satan* in the park bookstore.[43] I'm with him.

Every attempt to remove this constitutionally offensive material from the bookstore during Bush's terms met with typical Bushian stubbornness. The presidents of the American Geological Institute and six of its member societies as well as the Public Employees for Environmental Responsibility organization fought this creationist title for years. All that happened was that the creationist book was moved to the "inspirational" section of the bookstore.[44]

Yet in 2005 the National Parks Service approved a new policy on educational materials that said they must "be based on the best scientific evidence available, as found in scholarly sources that have stood the test of scientific peer review and criticism [and] interpretive and educational programs must refrain from appearing to endorse religious beliefs explaining natural processes."[45]

It's not just that the Republicans continue to take and argue ridiculous positions. It's that they're wildly, obviously, and unapologetically abusing the federal government to do it. The consequence has been a long-drawn-out, multiyear battle over something that is simply not arguable.

Abstinence-Only Education Does Not Work

In the time Bush was in office, from 2001 to 2008, the federal government directed about $1.5 billion to telling our children not to have sex, only to find that, in an unsurprising development, 88 percent of kids who have abstinence-only education still have premarital sex.[46]

THE RIGHT

"It is the will of God that you abstain from sexual impurity until you are married."[47]

WHY WE'RE RIGHT/THE SCIENCE

"A long-awaited national study has concluded that abstinence-only sex education, a cornerstone of the Bush administration's social agenda, does not keep teenagers from having sex. Neither does it increase or decrease the likelihood that if they do have sex, they will use a condom."[48]

For decades the Republicans have been pushing abstinence-only programs. In 1981, they passed the Adolescent Family Life Act (AFLA), which funded educational programs to "promote self-discipline and other prudent approaches" to adolescent sex, or "chastity education." In 1996, they took it a step further and used a welfare bill to establish a federal program to exclusively fund abstinence-only programs.[49]

President Bush has continued to follow the abstinence-only doctrine blindly. In his FY2008 budget, he requested $242 million in abstinence-only funding. Congress was right there with him. As the Obama administration came into office, it was faced with considering the fate of $176 million in annual funding for abstinence-only education.[50]

Representative Henry Waxman of California released a report in spring 2007 that exposed just how loony the curricula of abstinence-only programs in this country are. Of thirteen abstinence-only courses they analyzed, only two were not scientifically inaccurate. Of the eleven that were inaccurate, the fallacies weren't small—they were on the scale of two extra chromosomes, for example. That's the difference between species.[51]

Here are some of my other favorite errors in abstinence-only education from the Waxman Report or, as some might refer to it, sex according to the Bush administration:

Myth: HIV/AIDS is spread through sweat and tears.

Fact: According to the CDC, HIV is transmissible only through blood, semen, and vaginal secretions.

Myth: [R]esearch confirms that 14 percent of the women who use condoms scrupulously for birth control become pregnant within a year.

Fact: In fact, when used correctly and consistently, only 2 percent of couples who rely on the latex condom as their primary form of contraception will experience an unintended pregnancy.

Myth: Twenty-four chromosomes from the mother and twenty-four from the father join to create [a fetus].

Fact: Human cells are actually comprised of forty-six chromosomes; twenty-three from each parent.

When people in my family get sick, I like to get medical advice from a doctor, not a right-wing nut job. So that's who I'll turn to now for advice and pronouncements on this medically relevant topic. The doctors say, via the American Medical Association, that there is "no evidence that abstinence sex education works."[52]

Not only does abstinence-only education not work, it often results in unsafe sex practices: one study found that "There is little evidence that teens who participate in abstinence-only programs abstain from intercourse longer than others. It is known, however, that when they do become sexually active, teens who received abstinence-only education often fail to use condoms or other contraceptives. In fact, 88 percent of students who pledged virginity in middle school and high school still engage in premarital sex. The students who break this pledge are less likely to use contraception at first intercourse, *and* they have similar rates of sexually transmitted infections as non-pledgers."[53]

Defenders of this policy of abstinence-only education like to claim responsibility for a decline in teen pregnancy from 1995 to 2002. That decline, however, was only 14 percent due to abstinence and *86 percent* due to the use of contraception.[54] In other words, the decline in teen pregnancy was thanks to Clinton, not conservatives.

The only thing abstinence-only education does is load young people down with rather dangerous notions about sex and protection. For example, thinking that condoms are effective only two thirds of the time. (I'm not saying condoms are perfect, but they *are* 98 percent effective in preventing pregnancy when used correctly.)[55]

Abstinence-only education and related programs teach our kids that condoms and birth control pills don't work, which has the effect of leading them not to try to use anything at all when they have sex. They think there's no point. Hopefully, we can all recognize that this is not an acceptable trend.

Women's Health: The HPV Vaccine

THE RIGHT

"The seriousness of HPV and other STIs underscores the significance of God's design for sexuality to human well being. Thus, Focus on the Family affirms—above any available health intervention—abstinence until marriage and faithfulness after marriage as the best and primary practice in preventing HPV and other STIs."[56]

WHY WE'RE RIGHT/THE SCIENCE

"Studies have found the vaccine to be almost 100% effective in preventing diseases caused by the four HPV types covered by the vaccine—including pre-cancers of the cervix, vulva and vagina, and genital warts."[57]

The Centers for Disease Control and Prevention (CDC) has studied the HPV vaccine and concluded that it's almost 100 percent effective in preventing HPV. To be most effective the CDC reports that it needs to be administered before girls become sexually active and therefore should be administered for girls of eleven to twelve and as young as nine. The vaccine has been extensively studied by the FDA and is rated as "safe and effective," with no serious side effects.[58]

Republicans don't want young women to get the HPV vaccine because if they take it, they'll be less likely to get sick if they have sex, which, of course, means they'll keep having sex. The best response I've seen to the Republicans on this issue came from Katha Pollitt in *The Nation:*

Wonderful, you are probably thinking, all we need to do is vaccinate girls (and boys too for good measure) before they become sexually active, around puberty, and HPV—and, in thirty or forty years, seven in ten cases of cervical cancer—goes poof.

Not so fast: We're living in God's country now. The Christian right doesn't like the sound of this vaccine at all. "Giving the HPV vaccine to young women could be potentially harmful," Bridget Maher of the Family Research Council told the British magazine *New Scientist*, "because they may see it as a license to engage in premarital sex." Raise your hand if you think that what is keeping girls virgins now is the threat of getting cervical cancer when they are 60 from a disease they've probably never heard of.[59]

To paraphrase Ms. Pollitt's point, it seems rather unlikely that some seventeen-year-old girl in the backseat of a car who was considering having sex with her boyfriend that night would suddenly say, "Wait, hold on, I could get cervical cancer." It's been a somewhat long time since I was a teenager, but if memory serves me right, the threat of cervical cancer is not really looming large for many teenagers.

The lengths the Bush administration has gone to in order to sabotage women's health would be remarkable under any other president. For Bush, they are simply typical. When the Bush administration had a say in the makeup of an agency or panel, you could bet it was going to pack the panel with people as crazy as it was. Bush named a guy who said women should pray to relieve PMS to the FDA's Reproductive Health Drugs Advisory Commission.[60] I don't think I've asked my wife or any other female consultants about their success with combating cramps with prayer, but I can bet I know what their answer will be—and you can bet it won't be printable.

Being Gay Is Not a Choice

THE RIGHT

"I feel homosexuality is an aberrant, unnatural and sinful lifestyle."—Governor Mike Huckabee.[61]

WHY WE'RE RIGHT/THE SCIENCE

"The idea that sexual preference is a hard-wired part of who we are is consistent with a growing body of scientific research that indicates a biological basis for sexual orientation, including studies of identical twins, studies of other species that don't have cultural influences, and the discovery of genes that can change the sexual behavior in flies."[62]

There's no serious person who believes that being gay is a choice. The Republicans, and even some Democrats, are just plain wrong on this one. And it matters what people say, because public figures have sway. They affect what people think. People who think being gay is a choice are only about a quarter as likely to support gay rights as those who think being gay is a matter of birth—22 percent of people who think being gay is a choice support gay rights, but 78 percent of those who know that gay and straight are matters of birth support equal rights. It matters what people say, and it matters what we teach our children.[63]

During the 2004 election, CBS News anchor Bob Schieffer asked President Bush if he thought being gay is a choice. Bush replied, "You know, Bob, I don't know. I just don't know." Although it would be a somewhat tiring exercise to keep up with everything Bush doesn't know, and I try not to worry about most of it, this is something everyone should know: being gay isn't a choice. Here's the exchange.

> **SCHIEFFER:** Both of you are opposed to gay marriage. But to understand how you have come to that conclusion, I want to ask you a more basic question. Do you believe homosexuality is a choice?
>
> **BUSH:** You know, Bob, I don't know. I just don't know.[64]

It's no surprise that Bush had support from the rest of the right wing, and all the men who have hoped to succeed him (and didn't). When my friend the late Tim Russert cornered Governor Mike Huckabee on NBC's *Meet the Press* in 2007, he confronted Huckabee with his statement that "homosexuality is an aberrant, unnatural, and sinful lifestyle":

> **MR. RUSSERT:** But when you say aberrant or unnatural, do you believe you're born gay or you choose to be gay?

GOV. HUCKABEE: I don't know whether people are born that way. People who are gay say that they're born that way. But one thing I know, that the behavior one practices is a choice.[65]

I wonder how Governor Huckabee would take it if suddenly he faced elected officials saying on national television that they thought practicing heterosexuality was a sin.

Senator McCain, for his part, danced around the issue of gay rights throughout the primary and general election. He's said he's for and against civil marriage—during the same taping of *This Week*—and again during a single taping of *Hardball*.

MATTHEWS: Should there be—should gay marriage be allowed?

MCCAIN: I think—I think that gay marriage should be allowed if there's a ceremony kind of thing, if you want to call it that. I don't have any problem with that. But I do believe in preserving the sanctity of a union between man and woman.

Later during the show, McCain tacked a pivot on gay rights onto a response about the farm bill, correcting back to the right-wing position:

MCCAIN: . . . Could I just mention one other thing? On the issue of the gay marriage, I believe that if people want to have private ceremonies, that's fine. I do not believe that gay marriages should be legal.[66]

This right-wing craziness is not confined to Congress; Republicans are also busy inserting state governments in people's bedrooms. A majority of states have passed some form of legislation limiting or preventing people's right to get married.[67] It is disheartening to watch such legislation passing in states that vote Democratic.

Despite the right-wing hysteria, so far gay marriage has not destroyed the country. On May 17, 2004, Massachusetts officially recognized same sex-marriage.[68] Five years have passed and Massachusetts seems to be intact. If it has had trouble with apocalyptic events following the legalization of same-sex marriage, news hasn't reached New Orleans yet.

When it comes to the shrill protests and vile bigotry of the right wing, the only suggestion I can offer is to embrace your natural commonsense horror at the words of these right-wing bigots. It's hard to listen to Katherine Harris, who claims same-sex marriage would cause anarchy.[69] It's worse to hear the homophobic proclamations of former Senator Rick Santorum, who compares same-sex unions to "man on dog" relationships.[70]

RICK SANTORUM

AP: I mean, should we outlaw homosexuality?

SANTORUM: I have no problem with homosexuality. I have a problem with homosexual acts. As I would with acts of other, what I would consider to be, acts outside of traditional heterosexual relationships. And that includes a variety of different acts, not just homosexual. I have nothing, absolutely nothing against anyone who's homosexual. If that's their orientation, then I accept that. And I have no problem with someone who has other orientations. The question is, do you act upon those orientations? So it's not the person, it's the person's actions. And you have to separate the person from their actions.

AP: OK, without being too gory or graphic, so if somebody is homosexual, you would argue that they should not have sex?

SANTORUM: We have laws in states, like the one at the Supreme Court right now, that has sodomy laws and they were there for a purpose. Because, again, I would argue, they undermine the basic tenets of our society and the family. And if the Supreme Court says that you have the right to consensual sex within your home, then you have the right to bigamy, you have the right to polygamy, you have the right to incest, you have the right to adultery. You have the right to anything. Does that undermine the fabric of our society? I would argue yes, it does. . . . Every society in the history of man has upheld the institution of marriage as a bond between a man and a woman. Why? Because society is based on one thing: that society is based on the future of the society. And that's what? Children. Monogamous relationships. In every society, the definition of marriage has not ever to my knowledge included homosexuality. That's not to pick on homosexuality. It's not, you know, man on child, man on dog, or whatever the case may be.[71]

Republican claims that gay marriage and gay rights undermine the fabric of society are absurd. As the physicist Wolfgang Pauli used to say about ill-reasoned papers, these claims are "not even wrong." They're too far outside the realm of rationality to even dignify with a response.

Fortunately there are commonsense Democrats fighting back against this hatred and bigotry by introducing legislation to repeal the military's ineffective "Don't Ask, Don't Tell" policy and to prohibit discrimination based on sexual orientation.[72]

The Republicans Stole Florida

Gore won Florida in 2000. The Republicans stole Florida. Period, end of the story. I'm never going to get over that. And I'm never going to stop saying that (see Chapter 3).

THE RIGHT

They took Florida.

WHY WE'RE RIGHT/THE MATH

The Florida vote was tainted by a series of errors and political interpretations. Under a full accounting, Gore most likely would be president.

Oh, the Books They'll Write: Scott McClellan and Other Administration Defectors

The fuss last year over Scott McClellan's book would make you think it was the first time a Bush loyalist defected. Wrong. McClellan's wasn't the first book about this administration, and it won't be the last. There are a lot of unanswered questions. Members of the Bush administration may be out of office, but they're going to be dealing with tell-all books and congressional investigations for the rest of their lives. There will be more books. Under the Obama administration, I hope and pray and expect there will be investigations. Congress will chase down answers to a number of open questions about the war in Iraq and the unprecedented financial meltdown, among other things. Historians will launch their own full investigations. President Bush and this administration will spend a long, long time defending what was done and answering for their actions.

The National Opinion Research Center (NORC) at the University of Chicago was hired by a consortium on media outlets to conduct the definitive study on who won the disputed Florida election. NORC concluded that, "under a full accounting, Gore most likely would be president."[73] Republicans can kick and scream, but this study—again, from the University of Chicago, not exactly a reliable liberal stronghold—uses hard math and facts.

There were many factors and improper actions pushed by Bush's Republican cronies in Florida that combined to steal the election from Al Gore.

Republican election officials improperly allowed questionable absentee ballots, mainly from Bush-leaning counties, giving him 292 votes. Suspicious and confusing ballot designs were used in Palm Beach and Duval County, which are heavily populated by seniors citizens who vote predominantly Democratic. These ballots were not counted and cost Gore approximately 113,000 votes. Older voting machines were also used in areas that were heavily populated by seniors, African-Americans, and lower-income voters who favor Democrats, and these errors cost Gore an additional 120,000 votes.[74]

Not to mention that the U.S. Civil Rights Commission concluded that Katherine Harris and the Republican election officials had improperly scrubbed voting rolls of "felons," 180,000 of whom were legally able to vote. Of those excluded, 54 percent were African-Americans who vote overwhelmingly Democratic.[75]

The facts are clear: Al Gore won. For my Republican friends who will whine, "Oh, it's in the past," or, "Get over it," I say, look at what the past eight years have brought. Go talk to the families of thousands of soldiers who are dead or maimed. Go talk to the people of New Orleans whose lives are still devastated after Katrina. Go talk to the millions of Americans living in poverty.

Ask them if they are over it. I know I'm not. The only thing that's over is the argument of the inarguable, of issues that are *res judicata*.

CHAPTER 9

Just the Facts, Ma'am

Like most Americans, I'm sick of Democrats and Republicans. Ultimately, although I do want to see Democrats in office, I don't want to hear "liberal" or "conservative" ever again. I don't want any more ideology, just evidence. Obama's "post-partisan," "post-racial" campaign was pretty much perfectly timed to appeal to the wide body of Americans who are absolutely sick of "red" states and "blue" states and partisan warfare.

We don't have to choose between the government and the market. It's an idiotic false choice we've engrained in our political system. All over the world you have countries with both free markets and nationalized health care, for example. What do England, Canada, Japan, and Singapore have in common? A stock market and national health care.

We can even favor a strong military without advocating ill-planned wars. And, finally, and please remember this one, we don't have to choose between the Constitution and fighting terrorism. Yet, historically speaking, both parties keep returning to the same asinine positions over and over again, and we keep debating them.

Both parties have become anchored to their share of senseless positions and expect the same of their members. Why is it that if someone is pro-choice, she has to be for gun control? The two don't have anything to do with each other. And though conventional partisan politics dictates that if you're for national health insurance, you're for protectionist economic policy, I don't buy it. The truth of the matter is that protectionism doesn't work.

Yet the parties keep sticking to their absurd divisions and up-
dating their partisanship-based attacks. The Republicans say that
the Democrats are closer than they'll admit to corporate interests
and were too quick to go along with what they called an unwise
and unjust war. The Democrats accuse the Republican Party of being too far from the people and too close to a far right Christian
fringe.

They're both right, and they're both wrong. I mean to say that
they both have a point, but they both miss the point. Politics right
now isn't about ideology or parties anymore. It's about policy that
works. So let's coin a new word. I'm an evidencist. If there's evidence that a policy works as it should, and that it benefits the public good, I'll be for it.

It's not like we haven't accumulated an entire body of knowledge about what things work and don't work in American politics.
I'm for the New York Stock Exchange and the NASDAQ, and I'm
for increasing funding to schools. I'm for strong military, and I'm
against the Iraq War. I'm for well-reasoned, thought-out positions.

The most pathetic of all of these Washington types are people,
like those on *The Washington Post* editorial page, who try to be
moderate for the sake of being moderate. Think Joe Lieberman or
even Dick Morris. Morris picks the middle between two positions
because, in his mind, if both sides are against it, it must be good.
That is the worst logic in the world.

Radically enough, I'm going to suggest that we should be considering policy based on, well, the merit of the policy. Here are the
options: we know this is good policy; we think it's good policy;
we're not sure; we think it's bad policy; or we know it's bad policy.
Whether or not we support policy should have nothing to do with
its place on an ideological continuum.

Later on, once we're arguing about good policies, we can turn to
ideology. Where we've got a legitimate dividing point—one certainly worth arguing over and flushing out—is over how much the
government should be doing. It's my firm belief that government
should do everything that it can for people who are trying to make

it rather than people who already have it made. In my first book I used the term "5-65 Democrat."

The concept of a 5-65 Democrat comes from my mother's axiom that there are only two acceptable things for people between the ages of five and sixty-five in this world to do: be training for a job or in a job. The federal government's role is to do everything it can to encourage people between these ages to train for and be employed in work. I'm probably less enamored of welfare than many progressives, but I'm much more enamored of concepts like education, unemployment compensation, and universal health care.

Truth be told, I don't even really think that arguing over social policy spending should have that much to do with ideology. Helping people get educated and find work eliminates poverty and reduces the income gap, which is to say, it makes things better in the country as a whole.

So please, if you're asked to describe your political ideology, say you're an evidencist with a general sympathy toward people who are struggling to get ahead. Hotel maids, small businesspeople, policemen, teachers, salespeople, you name it. From now on I want to be an evidencist. It's my high hope that Obama continues on his own refreshingly post-partisan, post-ideological course.

CHAPTER 10

Spike the Ball: Truman-Carville-Bartels vs. Limbaugh-Gingrich-Bush*

Over many years of engaging in as much political debate as anybody in Washington, I've come to realize that on a lot of issues, the other side has a point. By and large, I think the side that Democrats and progressives are on is better than the side that Republicans and conservatives are on. But who knows? Maybe Republicans have a point on some of these educational issues. Maybe they have a point on crime. (It'll surprise no one that I occasionally tend to agree with them on things like that.)

We always thought that we had a better point on the economy, but we thought they might have a point, too. It seemed like the best argument we made was that their policies might make for a better economy, but our progressive policies make for a better society. In short, aren't you willing to give up something in the economy to achieve something for society? For a long time that constituted the underlying progressive, Democratic argument.

I'm very proud to say that in 1996 in *We're Right, They're Wrong,*

---

* Because the book-writing process takes time and the full extent of the Bush administration's failures on the economy has yet to be reported, even the searing indictment you'll read in the pages that follow will be grotesquely understated.

112

I actually took a look at economic performance under Democrats and Republicans and concluded that Democrats had not only produced a more just society but, according to my amateur and partisan analysis, actually produced a better economy.

Much as I'm examining the disastrous legacy of the Bush administration today, James Carville circa 1996 autopsied the Reagan economy:

By the time he rode off into the sunset, Reagan had racked up almost $2 trillion in debt. Let's forget for a minute the fact that $2 trillion of deficit spending was what allowed Reagan to post economic growth. Let's just look at what a hole that debt put us in. If it weren't for all the interest we're paying on the debt he and his Vice President ran up—it's costing us some $180 billion in interest this year alone—we'd be in the black right now. Let me state that another way: if we didn't have to deal with the Reagan-Bush debt, we wouldn't be arguing over how and when to balance the budget. We'd already have a balanced budget. Reagan also promised us economic growth like we'd never seen before. But take a look at the books: We got slower growth in the 1980s than we had in the 1970s. He promised that his tax cuts on the rich would lead to unprecedented growth in our productivity and savings. Wrong. Productivity growth was pathetically anemic, and our savings rate plummeted.[1]

More than that, thirteen years ago, we already knew that supply-side economics in particular was, not to put too fine a point on it, a load of crap.

It's not hard to figure out what went wrong. A handful of goofballs convinced Reagan to experiment with an untested concept called supply-side economics. It was the economic equivalent of jumping off the roof with an umbrella for a parachute—and instead of a busted ass, we got a busted treasury.[2]

That's still right, and they're still wrong. Unfortunately, Reagan's experiment with an untested theory and its clear, disastrous repercussions weren't enough to kill the rumor of conservative superiority on the economy.

Although *We're Right, They're Wrong* achieved some commercial success—it did reach number 1 on the *New York Times* Best Sellers list, I'm proud to say—its impact on the Washington elites could generously be described as minimal. After all, Carville is an uncouth, bigmouthed, partisan hack, a Clinton sycophant who is not schooled in the nuances of policy. And so your humble author had basically moved on. And while I myself considered my argument to be persuasive and correct, I had resigned myself to the fact that it was never going to make much of a dent in the way that the commentariat or the chin-scratchers really thought.

Then along came one Professor Larry M. Bartels of Princeton University, generally considered to be a reputable institution of learning. Mr. Bartels described himself as a person who had not even voted since 1984, in which election he actually voted for Ronald Reagan.

So, in comes Mr. Bartels, a man of pristine academic credentials and so non-partisan in his approach that he hadn't even voted in more than twenty years. And what did Mr. Bartels determine after exhaustive and relentless study of the U.S. economy under Democratic and Republican presidents? He discovered—well, how do I put this modestly?—he discovered that James Carville was right twelve years ago. It is truly a testament to America that a humble Cajun boy, of very modest academic achievements and limited attention span, could actually have postulated a theory in 1996 that is completely validated by this seminal work.

It has now been stated, clearly and with the weight of Ivy League bona fides, that not only did Democrats build a more just society, they far and away built a better economy. I wish I could take credit for being the originator of this hypothesis, but that would have to go to another Democrat, who was also decried as a bumpkin by the David Broders of that day. That would be former President Harry

S Truman. It was Truman who so brilliantly observed that "if you want to live like a Republican, you have to vote like a Democrat."

What you see is that the Truman-Carville-Bartels position is the economic equivalent of evolution, while the Limbaugh-Gingrich-Reagan-Bush stance is the economic equivalent of creationism.

So, all of you who have listened to their nauseating claptrap about marginal rates, the death tax, regulation stifling economic growth, trickle-down, supply-side, and every other piece of idiotic tripe you had to endure at every boring cocktail party, join me in breaking out a bottle of good champagne and giving yourself a toast, because you don't just stand for justice—you stand with the facts. Congratulations to the Democratic Party for winning on all measures of both economic growth and social justice.

Democrats Do It Better

The truth is, since 1900 Democratic presidents have dominated on every economic front.

Let's do a quick rundown of the presidential scorecard. The dissection of more than a hundred years of White House economic policy reveals some startling if not unexpected numbers:

- Since 1900, Democrats saw a 12.3 percent return on the S&P 500 to the Republicans' 8 percent
- Since 1930, Democrats created 5.4 percent GDP growth. Republicans rang in with only 1.6 percent.[3]

Do I need to keep going?

Don't take it from me. I'll turn the floor over to the good people of the *Los Angeles Times*, the *Washington Monthly*, and Princeton University, for a cross section.

In April 2005, Michael Kinsley did a quick rundown of spending, deficit, GDP, and unemployment for the *Los Angeles Times*. Kinsley started with the 1960 Economic Report and used forty-five years of economic history to debunk the Republicans' claims to smaller government:

Consider federal spending (a.k.a. "big government"). It has gone up an average of about $50 billion a year under presidents of both parties. But that breaks down as $35 billion a year under Democratic presidents and $60 billion under Republicans. If you assume that it takes a year for a president's policies to take effect (so, for example, President Clinton is responsible for 2001 and George W. Bush takes over in 2002), Democrats have raised spending by $40 billion a year and Republicans by $55 billion.[4]

Then, in May 2005, Kevin Drum followed up on Kinsley's math in the *Washington Monthly*. Drum's conclusion was essentially "spike the ball." It's done. Game, set, match. He wrote:

The results are simple: Democratic presidents have consistently higher economic growth and consistently lower unemployment than Republican presidents. If you add in a time lag, you get the same result. If you eliminate the best and worst presidents, you get the same result. If you take a look at other economic indicators, you get the same result. There's just no way around it: Democratic administrations are better for the economy than Republican administrations.[5]

FIGURE 1

Macroeconomic Performance under Democratic and Republican Presidents, 1948–2005

Average values of macroeconomic indicators (with standard errors in parentheses). Partisan control measured from one year following inauguration to one year following subsequent inauguration.

	All Presidents	Democratic Presidents	Republican Presidents	Partisan Difference
Unemployment (%)	5.63 (.19)	4.84 (.24)	6.26 (.24)	−1.42 (.34)
Inflation (%)	3.85 (.39)	3.97 (.71)	3.76 (.43)	.20 (.80)
Real per capita GNP growth (%)	2.15 (.31)	2.78 (.41)	1.64 (.43)	1.14 (.60)
N	58	26	32	58

SOURCE: CALCULATIONS BASED ON DATA FROM BUREAU OF LABOR STATISTICS AND BUREAU OF ECONOMIC ANALYSIS

FIGURE 2

Macroeconomic Performance under Democratic
and Republican Presidents, 1948–2005

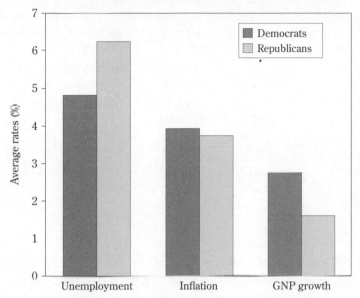

SOURCE: BARTELS, LARRY M.; UNEQUAL DEMOCRACY. © 2008 BY RUSSELL SAGE
FOUNDATION. PUBLISHED BY PRINCETON UNIVERSITY PRESS. REPRINTED BY
PERMISSION OF PRINCETON UNIVERSITY PRESS.

Democrats are also indisputably better for social justice. Two
words for you: income inequality.

Under Democrats, income inequality declines. Under Republicans, it grows. Back in 2004, Bartels wrote, "My projections suggest that income inequality . . . would actually have *declined* slightly
over the past thirty years had the patterns of income growth actually observed during Democratic administrations been in effect
throughout that period; conversely, continuous application of the
patterns of income growth actually observed during periods of
Republican control would have produced an even greater diver-
gence in the economic fortunes of rich and poor" [italics added].[6]
Republican policies would create what Bartels calls a "Platinum-
Gilded Age."[7]

In 2008, Bartels came up with a graph to prove it.

FIGURE 3

Real Income Growth Rates by Income Level and
Presidential Partisanship, 1948–2005

Average annual real pre-tax income growth (%) for families at various points in the income distribution (with standard errors in parentheses). Partisan control measured from one year following inauguration to one year following subsequent inauguration.

	All Presidents	Democratic Presidents	Republican Presidents	Partisan Difference
20th percentile	1.42 (.50)	2.64 (.77)	.43 (.61)	2.21 (.97)
40th percentile	1.54 (.39)	2.46 (.58)	.80 (.49)	1.67 (.75)
60th percentile	1.73 (.34)	2.47 (.52)	1.13 (.43)	1.33 (.67)
80th percentile	1.84 (.33)	2.38 (.50)	1.39 (.42)	.99 (.65)
95th percentile	2.00 (.38)	2.12 (.65)	1.90 (.46)	.22 (.77)
N	58	26	32	58

SOURCE: BARTELS, LARRY M.; UNEQUAL DEMOCRACY. © 2008 BY RUSSELL SAGE FOUNDATION. PUBLISHED BY PRINCETON UNIVERSITY PRESS. REPRINTED BY PERMISSION OF PRINCETON UNIVERSITY PRESS.

The body of evidence against Republican economic policy has been a long time in growing. But now we have a damning compendium of commonsense observation, such as that provided by your humble author back in 1996, as well as Ivy League analysis and an unprecedented financial crisis with which to indict the Republicans.

The major economic policies of Republican presidents have all been resounding failures. You can just look back to *We're Right, They're Wrong* if you have any lingering doubts about trickle-down and supply-side economics—keep reading, to the final chapter, The Real Deal, for more of Carville's thoughts on the history of Republican economic policy.

Clinton vs. Bush

Allow me to introduce you to the perfect case study for Democratic superiority on the economy: Clinton vs. Bush. I may bear a slight bias, but the fact stands: the Clinton economy was stronger on every measure than Bush's has been. (In four years, when I write my next book, this chapter will chronicle the superior performance of Obama economic policies over Bushian economics.)

FIGURE 4

The Impact of Partisan Turnover on Partisan Differences in Real Income Growth Rates, 1948–2005

Average annual real pre-tax income growth (%) for families at various points in the income distribution (with standard errors in parentheses). Partisan control measured from one year following inauguration to one year following subsequent inauguration. "Partisan turnover" refers to first-term Democrats who succeeded Republicans or first-term Republicans who succeeded Democrats.

	All Presidents	Democratic Presidents	Republican Presidents	Partisan Difference
Partisan turnover				
20th percentile	1.38 (.75)	2.28 (1.00)	.71 (1.08)	1.57 (1.52)
40th percentile	1.52 (.54)	2.07 (.75)	1.11 (.76)	.96 (1.09)
60th percentile	1.60 (.47)	2.00 (.63)	1.30 (.67)	.71 (.95)
80th percentile	1.80 (.45)	2.19 (.62)	1.51 (.63)	.68 (.91)
95th percentile	1.89 (.45)	1.93 (.69)	1.86 (.61)	.07 (.92)
N	28	12	16	28
No Partisan turnover				
20th percentile	1.46 (.68)	2.95 (1.19)	.16 (.61)	2.80 (1.29)
40th percentile	1.56 (.56)	2.80 (.88)	.48 (.63)	2.31 (1.06)
60th percentile	1.86 (.51)	2.86 (.82)	1.97 (.57)	1.89 (.98)
80th percentile	1.87 (.48)	2.55 (.78)	1.27 (.57)	1.28 (.95)
95th percentile	2.10 (.62)	2.28 (1.07)	1.95 (.70)	.34 (1.25)
N	30	14	16	30

SOURCE: BARTELS, LARRY M.; UNEQUAL DEMOCRACY. © 2008 BY RUSSELL SAGE FOUNDATION. PUBLISHED BY PRINCETON UNIVERSITY PRESS. REPRINTED BY PERMISSION OF PRINCETON UNIVERSITY PRESS.

Bush Republicans have been trying to tear down the Clinton economy since Bush became the president-select in 2000, courtesy of five thieves in black robes, as my friend Paul Begala rightly refers to them. Their rhetoric falls flat in the face of fact. Just look at the fight I had back in 2000 with Oliver North on MSNBC:

NORTH: . . . It strikes me that what we've got is an economy that in the Marines we would say, "This economy is in a route the wrong way." What you've done is you're handing to the incoming administration an economy that's on a downward spiral, contracting, and going to make it more difficult for them.

CARVILLE: Wait a minute, when this administration took officc, the unemployment rate was 7.1. . . . The unemployment rate is 4.6 percent . . .

NORTH: Today.

CARVILLE: I'm saying where it is. The Dow is at 10,300 . . .

NORTH: Today.

CARVILLE: . . . 400, it went up today. You know where it was when he took office?

NORTH: Today . . . you guys are stuck in ancient history.

CARVILLE: What are you talking about? Excuse me . . .

NORTH: We're talking about today.

CARVILLE: . . . I'm telling you, put a 10,400 Dow in context, it was 3,200 when we took office. You put a 4.6 unemployment rate, you have to put it in context.

NORTH: James, let's look at a couple of leading indicators right now. New home starts, down. New car sales, down. Capital investment equipment, down.

CARVILLE: All of this is down from what? Down from what?

NORTH: Down from six months ago.

CARVILLE: But again, they're still growing. Every blue chip has between two-and-a-half and three-and-a-half percent growth. We were talking about when the Clinton administration took office you couldn't grow faster than two-and-a-half percent because you would overheat the economy. You know, it's like it's OK. Everybody gets it. We get a guy who comes into office. He wasn't elected. He was selected by five people. And he comes into office and the first thing he starts doing is trashing the best economy we've ever had in the history of the United States. If that's what he wants to say, if that's what he wants to run, if he wants to be the president of negativism, let him go. I mean, he's the president-select.[8]

North gave it a go, but it's hard to argue with numbers, even for Republicans.

At the end of Clinton's first term, the *New York Times* was reporting that "In the United States, economic growth was the best

FIGURE 5

Family Incomes by Income Percentile, 1947–2005

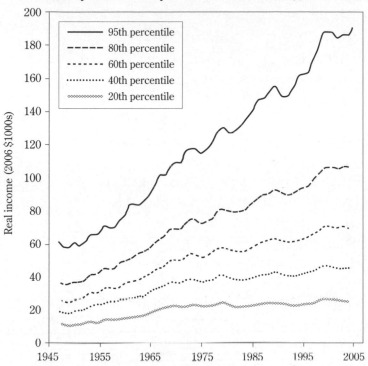

SOURCE: BARTELS, LARRY M.; UNEQUAL DEMOCRACY. © 2008 BY RUSSELL SAGE
FOUNDATION. PUBLISHED BY PRINCETON UNIVERSITY PRESS. REPRINTED BY
PERMISSION OF PRINCETON UNIVERSITY PRESS.

in a decade."[9] By the end of Clinton's second term, CNN joyfully announced: "Budget surpluses have surpassed most projections recently as the booming U.S. economy, now in its ninth year of expansion, and big stock market gains have filled government coffers with soaring revenues."[10]

It's no surprise that the Republicans tried to tear down Clinton's reputation and set some low expectations for the next four years. In fact, it was downright sensible. Unfortunately for the Republicans, there's no way to set expectations low enough for Bush. Just review the commentary on the U.S. economy in 2008, as Bush was preparing to leave the White House. If there's a stronger contrast than that between the reporting on the end of the Clinton economy

FIGURE 6

Top Incomes by Income Percentile, 1947–2005

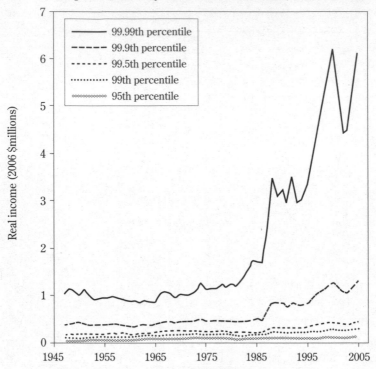

SOURCE: BARTELS, LARRY M.; UNEQUAL DEMOCRACY. © 2008 BY RUSSELL SAGE
FOUNDATION. PUBLISHED BY PRINCETON UNIVERSITY PRESS. REPRINTED BY
PERMISSION OF PRINCETON UNIVERSITY PRESS.

and from the last months of Bush, I don't know of it. After all, Clinton left us with the largest surplus in U.S. history.[11] Bush gave us a recession.

Here's what the experts said early in 2008, while Bush was still denying that the economy was in trouble:

> "The economy is now in a recession. . . . It will last longer and be deeper than the last two recessions, which lasted only 8 months from peak to trough. It could well be longer and deeper than the recession in the early 1980s that lasted 16 months"—Martin Feldstein, Harvard Professor of Economics and president of the National Bureau of Economic Research.[12]

FIGURE 7

Income Shares of Top 5 percent and
Top 1 percent, 1917–2005

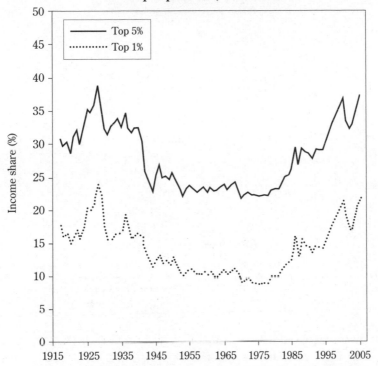

SOURCE: BARTELS, LARRY M.; UNEQUAL DEMOCRACY. © 2008 BY RUSSELL SAGE
FOUNDATION. PUBLISHED BY PRINCETON UNIVERSITY PRESS. REPRINTED BY
PERMISSION OF PRINCETON UNIVERSITY PRESS.

"I think it is a virtual certainty that the economic situation
will feel more like a recession on January 20, 2009, than it does
today. . . . From the perspective of Main Street and the real
economy, there is a very large amount of pain left to be felt"—
Larry Summers, former Treasury secretary and former president of Harvard University.[13]

It wasn't just a few Harvard economists, it was all the top minds
in economics.

Economists in the latest *Wall Street Journal* forecasting survey
are increasingly certain the U.S. has slid into recession, a view

FIGURE 8

Income Growth by Income Level under Democratic and Republican Presidents, 1948–2005

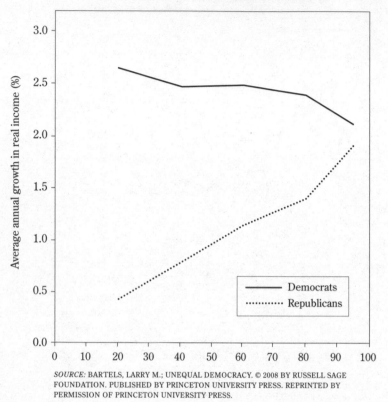

SOURCE: BARTELS, LARRY M.; UNEQUAL DEMOCRACY. © 2008 BY RUSSELL SAGE
FOUNDATION. PUBLISHED BY PRINCETON UNIVERSITY PRESS. REPRINTED BY
PERMISSION OF PRINCETON UNIVERSITY PRESS.

reinforced by new data showing a sharp drop in retail sales last month. "The evidence is now beyond a reasonable doubt," said Scott Anderson of Wells Fargo & Co. Thirty-six of 51 respondents, or more than 70%, said in a survey conducted March 7–11 that the economy is in recession.[14]

In case you needed a few more pieces of evidence, I'll direct you to not one but two former chairs of the Federal Reserve. There's Paul Volcker, who described the U.S. economic situation as "the mother of all crises."[15] Then there's the inimitable Alan Greenspan, who pronounced that "The current financial crisis in the U.S. is

FIGURE 9

Income Inequality under Democratic and Republican Presidents, 1947–2005

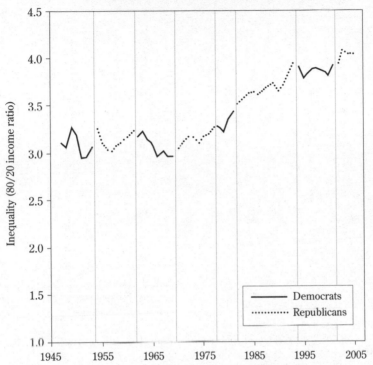

SOURCE: BARTELS, LARRY M.; UNEQUAL DEMOCRACY. © 2008 BY RUSSELL SAGE
FOUNDATION. PUBLISHED BY PRINCETON UNIVERSITY PRESS. REPRINTED BY
PERMISSION OF PRINCETON UNIVERSITY PRESS.

likely to be judged in retrospect as the most wrenching since the end of the second world war."[16]

Hold on a second—I'm going to have to ask you to read that again. Alan Greenspan said the current financial crisis will be "the most wrenching since the end of the second world war."

So, to review, Clinton exceeded all expectations for the U.S. economy to the positive and generated the largest budget surplus in U.S. history—and Bush took us back sixty years and engineered a recession.

FIGURE 10

Projected Income Inequality under Republican
and Democratic Presidents, 1947–2005

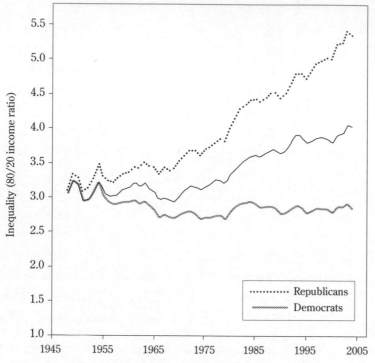

SOURCE: BARTELS, LARRY M.; UNEQUAL DEMOCRACY. © 2008 BY RUSSELL SAGE
FOUNDATION. PUBLISHED BY PRINCETON UNIVERSITY PRESS. REPRINTED BY
PERMISSION OF PRINCETON UNIVERSITY PRESS.

The Nitty-Gritty

Stick with me through the specifics. I'm going to keep harping on
the Bush economy vs. the Clinton economy for just a while longer.
I began comparing the two in *We're Right, They're Wrong*, and then
Paul Begala and I took a crack at it again in *Take It Back*. Using
hard facts to make Democrats and Republicans look bad wasn't
hard then. It's only gotten easier over the past few years.

Bush really has driven the economy into the ground. Going
back to Bartels for a moment, he produced what may be the single
funniest line in modern American political history. He quotes from

a study on income inequality from the predictably pretentious British magazine *The Economist*:

> Thanks to a jump in productivity growth after 1995, America's economy has outpaced other rich countries' for a decade. Its workers now produce over 30% more each hour they work more than ten years ago. In the late 1990s everybody shared in this boom. Though incomes were rising fastest at the top, all workers' wages far outpaced inflation.
>
> But after 2000 something changed. The pace of productivity growth has been rising again, but now it seems to be lifting fewer boats. . . . The fruits of productivity gains have been skewed towards the highest earners, and towards companies, whose profits have reached record levels as a share of GDP.[17]

Read that first line of the second paragraph again: "after 2000 something changed." Bartels gave a very dry, very academic response: "the report provided no hint of what 'something' might have changed after 2000."[18] What a killer line. An unnamed something happened after 2000.

Stock Market

Let's look at the Standard & Poor's 500 through December 2006. Under Clinton, it rose a whopping 207 percent. Bush managed to eke out 6 percent by the end of 2006, then there was the summer of 2008 and the stock market crash.[19] You'd think this would be enough to discourage Republicans from ever making a claim about stock market superiority again. Characteristically, they are ignoring the facts. The Republicans continue to claim that the Bush administration saw record highs in the S&P. Let's look a little more closely at these claims.

The Republican claim is that on July 19, 2007, the S&P 500 hit a "record high."[20] David Leonhardt of the *New York Times* points out that "the S&P remain[ed] 17 percent below its inflation-adjusted 2000 peak. A share in a mutual fund tied to the S&P 500, in other words, couldn't buy nearly as much then as it could in early 2000."[21] Record high? They didn't even break even.

Jobs

Clinton created 23 million jobs. Bush created only 5.6 million in his first six years.[22] In percentages, jobs increased by 2.38 percent per year under Clinton and decreased by 0.17 percent each year from 2000 to 2004 with Bush.[23] Put another way, Bush had the worst job creation record of the last seventy years—he added only 3.7 million non-farm jobs.[24]

The other problem is the type of jobs Bush created. Clinton produced full-time jobs, the type with benefits like health insurance. Under Clinton, the number of full-time jobs relative to part-time jobs rose. In the Bush economy, by contrast, job creation generated more part-time jobs. From 2001 to 2004, the ratio of full-time to part-time work declined at a rate of 1.67 percent.[25]

FIGURE 11

Unemployment Rate

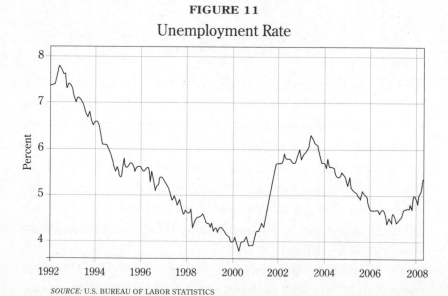

SOURCE: U.S. BUREAU OF LABOR STATISTICS

It's a favorite Republican trick to point to those few times Bush could claim lower levels of unemployment than Clinton. Not so fast, guys. Let's put this in context. Clinton came into office with 7.3 percent unemployment and lowered it to 4.2 percent. Bush, by comparison, managed to slightly increase the low unemployment he inherited, from 4.2 to 4.5 percent, and now Republicans have the audacity to claim that he did better than Clinton on unemployment.[26]

Wages/Income

In the Bush economy, incomes stagnated and the cost of living skyrocketed. "Raises" only helped people keep up with inflation.[27] Under Clinton, by the way, hourly earning rose by 6.8 percent. With Bush, there was only a 3.9 percent increase.[28]

Adjusted for inflation, the Bush minimum wage was $2.00/hr less than the Clinton minimum wage, despite the best efforts of congressional Democrats. The June 2007 minimum-wage increase wasn't really an increase. It only brought the minimum wage closer to its 1997 level. To actually increase the minimum wage, we'd have to raise it above $9.05/hr.[29]

Income stagnated and even fell under Bush. With Clinton, household income rose by $5,825 annually. Thanks to Bush, it decreased by $1,273. Poverty's up; health insurance is down. That income gap we started talking about in *We're Right, They're Wrong* is bigger than ever, and it's going to be one of Obama's biggest challenges to shrink it again.

Income Gap

Bill Clinton managed to work against income inequality. As one report put it, "Even in the highly inegalitarian economic climate of the 1990s, Bill Clinton managed to produce slightly stronger income growth for families at the 20th percentile (2.0 %) than at the 80th percentile (1.9%), though families at the very top of the income distribution did even better."[30]

Under Bush, the income of the top fifth of families grew more quickly than that of the middle fifths and far more quickly than that of the bottom fifth. It was not even really the whole top fifth. It was the top 5 percent of families. That 5 percent enjoyed increases in

FIGURE 12

People Below Poverty Level and Below 125 Percent of Poverty Level by Race and Hispanic Origin: 1980 to 2006

[(29,272 represents 29,272,000.) **People as of March of the following year.** Based on Current Population Survey, Annual Social and Economic Supplement (ASEC); See text, Section 1, and Appendix III. For data collection changes over time, see <http://www.census.gov/hhes/www/income/histinc/hstchg.html>]

Year	Number below poverty level (1,000)					Percent below poverty level					Below 125 percent of poverty level	
	All races [1]	White [2]	Black [3]	Asian and Pacific Islander [4]	His-panic [5]	All races [1]	White [2]	Black [3]	Asian and Pacific Islander [4]	His-panic [5]	Num-ber (1,000)	Percent of total popu-lation
1980....	29,272	19,699	8,579	(NA)	3,491	13.0	10.2	32.5	(NA)	25.7	40,658	18.1
1985....	33,064	22,860	8,926	(NA)	5,236	14.0	11.4	31.3	(NA)	29.0	44,166	18.7
1986....	32,370	22,183	8,983	(NA)	5,117	13.6	11.0	31.1	(NA)	27.3	43,486	18.2
1987 [6]..	32,221	21,195	9,520	1,021	5,422	13.4	10.4	32.4	16.1	28.0	43,032	17.9
1988....	31,745	20,715	9,356	1,117	5,357	13.0	10.1	31.3	17.3	26.7	42,551	17.5
1989....	31,528	20,785	9,302	939	5,430	12.8	10.0	30.7	14.1	26.2	42,653	17.3
1990....	33,585	22,326	9,837	858	6,006	13.5	10.7	31.9	12.2	28.1	44,837	18.0
1991 [7]...	35,708	23,747	10,242	996	6,339	14.2	11.3	32.7	13.8	28.7	47,527	18.9
1992 [7]...	38,014	25,259	10,827	985	7,592	14.8	11.9	33.4	12.7	29.6	50,592	19.7
1993 [8]...	39,265	26,226	10,877	1,134	8,126	15.1	12.2	33.1	15.3	30.6	51,801	20.0
1994....	38,059	25,379	10,196	974	8,416	14.5	11.7	30.6	14.6	30.7	50,401	19.3
1995....	36,425	24,423	9,872	1,411	8,574	13.8	11.2	29.3	14.6	30.3	48,761	18.5
1996....	36,529	24,650	9,694	1,454	8,697	13.7	11.2	28.4	14.5	29.4	49,310	18.5
1997....	35,574	24,396	9,116	1,468	8,308	13.3	11.0	26.5	14.0	27.1	47,853	17.8
1998....	34,476	23,454	9,091	1,360	8,070	12.7	10.5	26.1	12.5	25.6	46,036	17.0
1999 [9]...	32,791	22,169	8,441	1,285	7,876	11.9	9.8	23.6	10.7	22.7	45,030	16.3
2000 [10]..	31,581	21,645	7,982	1,258	7,747	11.3	9.5	22.5	9.9	21.5	43,612	15.6
2001 [11]..	32,907	22,739	8,136	1,275	7,997	11.7	9.9	22.7	10.2	21.4	45,320	16.1
2002 [11]..	34,570	23,466	8,602	1,161	8,555	12.1	10.2	24.1	10.1	21.8	47,084	16.5
2003....	35,861	24,272	8,781	1,401	9,051	12.5	10.5	24.4	11.8	22.5	48,687	16.9
2004 [12]..	37,040	25,327	9,014	1,201	9,122	12.7	10.8	24.7	9.8	21.9	49,693	17.1
2005....	36,950	24,872	9,168	1,402	9,368	12.6	10.6	24.9	11.1	21.8	49,327	16.8
2006....	36,460	24,416	9,048	1,353	9,243	12.3	10.3	24.3	10.3	20.6	49,688	16.8

NA Not available. [1]Includes other races not shown separately. [2]Beginning 2002, data represent White alone, which refers to people who reported White and did not report any other race category. [3]Beginning 2002, data represent Black alone, which refers to people who reported Black and did not report any other race category. [4]Beginning 2002, data represent Asian alone, which refers to people who reported Asian and did not report any other race category. [5]People of Hispanic origin may be of any race. [6]Implementation of a new March CPS processing system. [7]Implementation of 1990 census population controls. [8]The March 1994 income supplement was revised to allow for the coding of different income amounts on selected questionnaire items. Limits either increased or decreased in the following categories: earnings increased to $999,999; social security increased to $49,999; supplemental security income and public assistance increased to $24,999; veterans' benefits increased to $99,999; child support and alimony decreased to $49,999. [9]Implementation of Census 2000-based population controls. [10]Implementation of sample expansion by 28,000 households. [11]Beginning with the 2003 Current Population Survey (CPS), the questionnaire allowed respondents to choose more than one race. For 2002 and later, data represent persons who selected this race group only and exclude persons reporting more than one race. The CPS in prior years allowed respondents to report only one race group. [12]Data have been revised to reflect a correction to the weights in the 2005 ASEC.

SOURCE: U.S. CENSUS BUREAU, CURRENT POPULATION REPORTS, P60–233; AND INTERNET SITES <HTTP://WWW.CENSUS .GOV/PROD/2007PUBS/P60–233.PDF>(RELEASED AUGUST 2007) AND <HTTP://WWW.CENSUS.GOV/HHES/WWW/POVERTY/ HISTPOV/PERINDEX.HTML>.

income somewhere between 66 and 132 percent from the 1980s to 2000s. By comparison, the bottom fifth saw income growth of only 11 to 24 percent in the same states.[31]

Here's a table from the U.S. Census Bureau showing poverty rates from 1980 onward. I invite you, dear reader, to examine the decline in the number of people living below the poverty level between 1992 and 2000—3.5 percent. Then turn your gaze over to

FIGURE 13

Children Below Poverty Level by Race and Hispanic Origin: 1980 to 2006

[11,114 represents 11,114,000. Persons as of March of the following year. Covers only related children in families under 18 years old. Based on Current Population Survey; see text, this section and Section 1, and Appendix III. For data collection changes over time, see <http://www.census.gov/hhes/www/income/histinc/hstchg.html>]

Year	Number below poverty level (1,000)					Percent below poverty level				
	All races[1]	White[2]	Black[3]	Asian and Pacific Islander[4]	His-panic[5]	All races[1]	White[2]	Black[3]	Asian and Pacific Islander[4]	His-panic[5]
1980	11,114	6,817	3,906	(NA)	1,718	17.9	13.4	42.1	(NA)	33.0
1985	12,483	7,000	4,057	(NA)	2,512	20.1	15.6	43.1	(NA)	39.6
1987 [6]	12,275	7,398	4,234	432	2,606	19.7	14.7	44.4	22.7	38.9
1988	11,935	7,095	4,148	458	2,576	19.0	14.0	42.8	23.5	37.3
1989	12,001	7,164	4,257	368	2,496	19.0	14.1	43.2	18.0	35.5
1990	12,715	7,696	4,412	356	2,750	19.9	15.1	44.2	17.0	37.7
1991	13,658	8,316	4,637	348	2,977	21.1	16.1	45.6	17.1	39.8
1992 [7]	14,521	8,752	5,015	352	3,440	21.6	16.5	46.3	16.0	39.0
1993 [8]	14,961	9,123	5,030	358	3,666	22.0	17.0	45.9	17.6	39.9
1994	14,610	8,826	4,787	308	3,956	21.2	16.3	43.3	17.9	41.1
1995	13,999	8,474	4,644	532	3,938	20.2	15.5	41.5	18.6	39.3
1996	13,764	8,488	4,411	553	4,090	19.8	15.5	39.5	19.1	39.9
1997	13,422	8,441	4,116	608	3,865	19.2	15.4	36.8	19.9	36.4
1998	12,845	7,935	4,073	542	3,670	18.3	14.4	36.4	17.5	33.6
1999 [9]	11,678	7,194	3,698	367	3,561	16.6	13.1	32.8	11.5	29.9
2000 [10]	11,005	6,834	3,495	407	3,342	15.6	12.4	30.9	12.5	27.6
2001	11,175	7,086	3,423	353	3,433	15.8	12.8	30.0	11.1	27.4
2002 [11]	11,646	7,203	3,570	302	3,653	16.3	13.1	32.1	11.4	28.2
2003	12,340	7,624	3,750	331	3,982	17.2	13.9	33.6	12.1	29.5
2004 [12]	12,473	7,876	3,702	265	3,985	17.3	14.3	33.4	9.4	28.6
2005	12,335	7,652	3,743	312	3,977	17.1	13.9	34.2	11.0	27.7
2006	12,299	7,522	3,690	351	3,959	16.9	13.6	33.0	12.0	26.6

NA Not available. [1]Includes other races not shown separately. [2]Beginning 2002, data represent White alone, which refers to people who reported White and did not report any other race category. [3]Beginning 2002, data represent Black alone, which refers to people who reported Black and did not report any other race category. [4]Beginning 2002, data represent Asian alone, which refers to people who reported Asian and did not report any other race category. [5]People of Hispanic origin may be of any race. [6]Implementation of a new March CPS processing system. [7]Implementation of 1990 census population controls. [8]The March 1994 income supplement was revised to allow for the coding of different income amounts on selected questionnaire items. Limits either increased or decreased in the following categories: earnings increased to $999,999; social security increased to $49,999; supplemental security income and public assistance increased to $24,999; veterans' benefits increased to $99,999; child support and alimony decreased to $49,999. [9] Implementation of Census 2000-based population controls. [10]Implementation of sample expansion to 28,000 households. [11]Beginning with the 2003 Current Population Survey (CPS), the questionnaire allowed respondents to choose more than one race. For 2002 and later, data represent persons who selected this race group only and excludes persons reporting more than one race. The CPS in prior years allowed respondents to report only one race group. [12]Data have been revised to reflect a correction to the weights in the 2005 Annual Social and Economic Supplement (ASEC).

SOURCE: U.S. CENSUS BUREAU, CURRENT POPULATION REPORTS, P60–233; AND INTERNET SITES <HTTP://WWW.CENSUS .GOV/PROD/2007PUBS/P60-233.PDF>(RELEASED AUGUST 2007) AND <HTTP://WWW.CENSUS.GOV/HHES/WWW/POVERTY/ HISTPOV/HSTPOV3.HTML>.

FIGURE 14

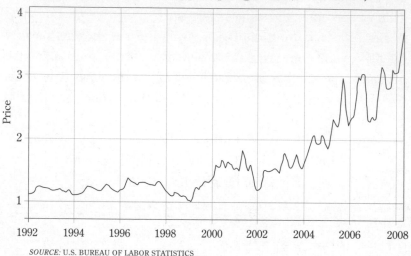

Price of Gasoline, all types, per gallon (3.785 liters)

SOURCE: U.S. BUREAU OF LABOR STATISTICS

that span between 2000 and 2005, and you'll find a 1.3 percent increase. Put another way, Clinton oversaw 6,433,000 people coming out of poverty and Bush put 5,369,000 Americans into poverty in just his first five years.[32]

Look at what happened to children. While Clinton was president, the number of children below the poverty line decreased. Under Bush, it increased.

People are working two jobs, children are sinking into poverty— and the Republicans tried to claim victory. Obama didn't let them get away with it, but now he's still left trying to fix the mess they've left behind.

Cost of Living

Income may not be increasing, but prices are. Take bread for an example. It's more than a third more expensive than it was in 2000.[33]

Here's the price of gas from 1992 to 2008. Notice the upward trend that begins in 2000:

Here's piped gas for utilities, like heat:

FIGURE 15

Price of Utility (Piped) Gas, 100 therms

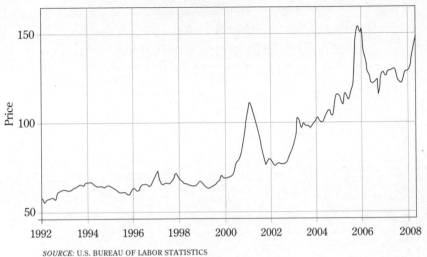

SOURCE: U.S. BUREAU OF LABOR STATISTICS

And here's fuel oil:

FIGURE 16

Price of Fuel Oil #2 per gallon (3.785 liters)

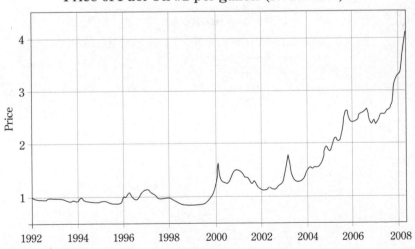

SOURCE: U.S. BUREAU OF LABOR STATISTICS

To get away from the energy theme for a bit, here's the price of bread:

FIGURE 17
Price of Bread, white, pan, per lb. (453.6 gm)

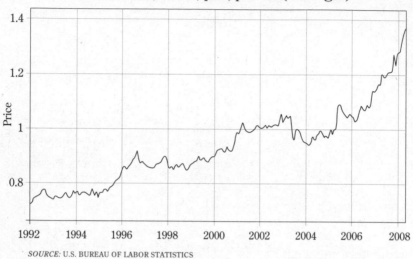

SOURCE: U.S. BUREAU OF LABOR STATISTICS

And now here's ground beef:

FIGURE 18
Price of Ground chuck, 100% beef, per lb. (453.6 gm)

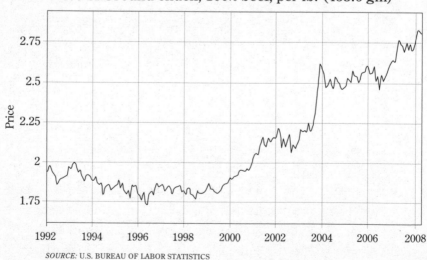

SOURCE: U.S. BUREAU OF LABOR STATISTICS

We're going to go into this one a little more when we get to young people. Right now the idea is just to give you a sense of how bleak the picture is.

Debt

The result of Bush's economic policies is rapidly growing personal and household debt. Going back to *Daily Kos* and a favorite of mine who writes there, Bonddad did some great work on debt in November 2007. He pointed out that "in the fourth quarter of 2001, total household debt was 75.10% of GDP. In the second quarter of 2007 it was 96.82%. . . . In the fourth quarter of 2001, total household debt was 102% of disposable income at the national level. In the second quarter of 2007 it was 129.62 % of personal income at the national level."[34]

The result goes back to the stock market. Bonddad rightly identifies soaring levels of debt as the force behind those early ominous headlines about the Wall Street giants taking huge losses. Think of the hits, one after another, that Citigroup, Merill Lynch, Morgan Stanley, Lehman Brothers, and the other big banks and brokerage houses took in fall 2007. The markets will not recover from this level of debt for years.

So, to sum it up, people are working more, earning less, and facing rising costs in every sector of the economy. Everything from health care to education to the price of bread has risen, and overall growth and wages aren't keeping up.

Fiscal Responsibility

Finally, let's look at fiscal responsibility. Bush managed to turn a $62.9 billion surplus into a deficit of $1.5 trillion. Public debt as a percentage of GDP fell 16.4 percent under Clinton, from 49.4 to 33 percent, only to rise back up to 38.5 percent during Bush's term.[35]

Need more? Our ratio of public debt to GDP—that is, the amount of debt the government owes relative to what we're making, the GDP—went up by almost a percentage point each year Bush has been in office. Surprise, surprise, it went down almost 4 percent annually under Clinton.[36]

So, then, what about trade? Here's another corner of economic performance where the Republicans would like to have you think they excel. Just ask Rush Limbaugh or Rudy Giuliani. I'm sure they'll be quick to point out that the trade deficit increased more rapidly under Clinton than Bush. So should we give No. 43 the win? Sure, unless you care about why and how the trade deficit rose during each administration.

Robert Atkinson and Julie Hutto of the Progressive Policy Institute explain:

> The trade deficit grew at the rate it did under Clinton for two main reasons: because the first Bush Administration's recession had cut imports to an artificially low level, and because the economy was expanding rapidly. People were confident, so they were buying a lot of imported goods. Businesses were growing, too, so U.S. factories were importing materials to manufacture their products. Throughout this period, export growth was very strong. In the Bush years, the trade deficit has been a product of a different, and less healthy dynamic: U.S. exports have dipped dramatically relative to imports.[37]

Clinton's record on every economic front and, indeed, for the whole of the expansion, exceeds Bush's by far. Period. Point, set, match. Republican manipulations of the numbers are wearing thin. People know the economy wasn't as strong under Bush. For any who'd like further evidence, I'd direct them to the nearest newspaper, gas station, or grocery store.

I can anticipate how the critics will feel about my using Democracy Corps numbers, so I'll give you Gallup instead. In December

2008, Gallup found that 78 percent of Americans were negative about the economy.[38]

Yet the Republicans keep repeating that everything is fine, like saying that Bush was a success economically will make it so. They are trying their damnedest to mislead people. They tried the same mumbo-jumbo in 2006, and it didn't work then, either. Republican strategist Frank Luntz told the *New York Times* right before the 2006 elections, "I don't know of another election cycle in which the economy was so good, yet the election prospects for the incumbent party looked so bad."[39]

Trust Dick Morris to come up with something even better in the lead-up to 2008. He claimed, "Bush's ratings on the economy are not bad, and he still draws commendations for his battle against terrorism."[40]

Morris should be used to being wrong, but this may be a new level of incorrect. Morris's statement flies in the face of every poll on Bush. Media Matters fact-checked Morris with the *Newsweek, Washington Post*/ABC, and *New York Times*/CBS News polls. *Newsweek*'s June 2007 survey showed that 60 percent of respondents disapproved of Bush's handling of the economy while only 34 percent approved. In the May–June 2007 *Washington Post*/ABC Poll, 57 percent disapproved and 40 approved. The *New York Times*/CBS News Poll offered little better news for Bush, with 56 percent disapproving and 36 approving.[41] A year later, in ARG's June 2008 survey, 71 percent disapproved and only 25 percent approved of Bush's handling of the economy.[42]

Of course the most egregious offenders when it comes to economic myths and lies were the Republican candidates. Usually people wait until an event is well in the past to revise it, but these guys attempted to rewrite history as it happened.

Exhibit A: The Republican primary, otherwise known as a caucus of reality-deniers. At the Republican debate in Michigan on October 9, 2007, Mitt Romney claimed that Michigan was alone in its economic downturn and that "the rest of the country is growing and seeing low levels of unemployment."[43]

Fred Thompson might have been worse. At the Michigan debate, he said, "I think if you look at the short term, it's rosy. I think if you look at a 10-year projection, it's rosy."[44] When Maria Bartiromo pressed him, citing the two thirds of Americans who said the country was in a recession or headed for one, Thompson responded with this winner:

Well, I think there are pockets in the economy. Certainly they're having difficulty. I think there are certainly those in Michigan that are having difficulty. I think you always find that in a vibrant, dynamic economy. I think that not enough has been done to tell what some call the greatest story never told, and that is that we are enjoying a period of growth right now, and we should acknowledge what got us there and continue those same policies on into the future.[45]

McCain similarly toed the Republican Party line, making only a tepid acknowledgment of America's economic plight. In October 2007, he still said only that the economy was "growing more slowly than anyone would like."[46]

The sole Republican candidate who seemed willing to own up to the coming crisis was Huckabee. It was Huckabee who warned at the Michigan debate, "I want to make sure people understand that for many people on this stage the economy's doing terrifically well, but for a lot of Americans it's not doing so well. The people who handle the bags and make the beds at our hotels and serve the food, many of them are having to work two jobs."[47]

The *Los Angeles Times* quoted Don Sipple on November 9, 2007, as saying that "Any economic pain comes out of the hide of the Republican Party."[48] That same article included a quote by Bill Whalen, formerly of the 1992 Bush reelection campaign and a fellow at the Hoover Institute. He warned, "What a weak economy does is, it lets the Democratic nominee go out and ask the Ronald Reagan question: Are you better off today than you were eight years ago?"[49]

Latinos in the Bush Economy

I'm just going to take a moment here to revisit a few of these numbers and tables with a special emphasis. Bush likes to make a lot of his supposed success with Latinos, but the truth is, Latinos are a Democratic group, and they're even more Democratic after this economic crisis. Few Americans did well under Bush, but some fared worse than others. Latinos were particularly hard-hit by the Bush economy.

- The **employment-population ratio** for Hispanics and Latinos dropped drastically when George W. Bush took office. Under Clinton, there was a 6.6 percent increase. Under Bush, there was a 0.8 percent decrease[50]
- The **unemployment rate** for Hispanics and Latinos decreased

FIGURE 19

Money Income of Families—Median Income by Race and Hispanic Origin in Current and Constant (2006) Dollars: 1990–2006

Year	Median income in current dollars					Median income in constant (2006) dollars				
	All families [1]	White [2]	Black [3]	Asian, Pacific Islander [4]	Hispanic [5]	All families [1]	White [2]	Black [3]	Asian, Pacific Islander [4]	Hispanic [5]
1990	35,353	36,915	21,423	42,246	23,431	52,869	55,205	32,037	63,177	35,040
1995 [6]	40,611	42,646	25,970	46,356	24,570	53,349	56,023	34,116	60,896	32,277
2000 [7, 8] ...	50,732	53,029	33,676	62,617	34,442	59,398	62,087	39,428	73,313	40,325
2001	51,407	54,067	33,598	60,158	34,490	58,545	61,574	38,263	68,511	39,279
2002 [9]	51,680	54,633	33,525	60,984	34,185	57,920	61,229	37,573	68,347	38,313
2003	52,680	55,768	34,369	63,251	34,272	57,751	61,136	37,677	69,340	37,571
2004 [10] ...	54,061	56,723	35,148	65,420	35,440	57,705	60,547	37,517	69,830	37,829
2005	56,194	59,317	35,464	68,957	37,867	58,036	61,262	36,627	71,218	39,109
2006	58,407	61,280	38,269	74,612	40,000	58,407	61,280	38,269	74,612	40,000

NA Not available. [1]Includes other races not shown separately. [2]Beginning with 2002, data represent White alone, which refers to people who reported White and did not report any other race category. [3]Beginning with 2002, data represent Black alone, which refers to people who reported Black and did not report any other race category. [4]Beginning with 2002, data represent Asian alone, which refers to people who reported Asian and did not report any other race category. [5]People of Hispanic origin may be of any race. [6]Data reflect full implementation of the 1990 census-based sample design and metropolitan definitions, 7,000 household sample reduction, and revised race edits. [7]Implementation of Census 2000-based population controls. [8]Implementation of a 28,000 household sample expansion. [9]See footnote 3, Table 673. [10]Data have been revised to reflect a correction to the weights in the 2005 ASEC.

SOURCE: U.S. CENSUS BUREAU, CURRENT POPULATION REPORTS, P60–233; AND INTERNET SITES <HTTP://WWW.CENSUS .GOV/PROD/2007PUBS /P60–233.PDF>(RELEASED AUGUST 2007) AND <HTTP://WWW.CENSUS.GOV/HHES/WWW/INCOME/ HISTINC/F05.HTML>.

under Clinton and drastically increased while Bush was in office

- **Median income** for Hispanics and Latinos in constant 2005 dollars increased under Clinton, but decreased under Bush.[51]

Median household income for Hispanics and Latinos sharply decreased under Bush, and sharply increased under Clinton.[52]

The percentage of Hispanics and Latinos below poverty level decreased by almost 10 percent under Clinton (1993–2000). It increased by 0.4 percent under Bush (2001–2005).[53]

The percentage of Hispanic children below poverty level decreased by 11.6 percent under Clinton (1993–2000) and increased by 0.3 percent under Bush (2001–2005).[54]

Spike the Ball

The Republicans have nothing left to claim on the economy. They have been weighed, measured, and found lacking by everyone from your author, James Carville, who barely graduated LSU, to Larry Bartels, who teaches at Princeton University, to the American people struggling with Bush's legacy of a rising cost of living and shrinking retirement.

The only recourse Republicans have left is to lie, and to hide the evidence of economic failure. That's just what they've tried to do. It's hard to hide grocery stores, banks, and gas pumps, but they're doing their best to bury the numerical evidence. The good news is, the Democrats—and the American people—aren't letting the Republicans get away with it this time.

In February 2008, as the mortgage crisis was getting worse and worse and it became clear a recession was looming, the Bush administration took action—by shutting down EconomicIndicators .gov, one of just a few solid sources of information about the U.S. economy available to the public. To give you an idea of how important this one Web site is, the *Wall Street Journal* described it as "a

FIGURE 20

Money Income of Households—Median Income by Race and Hispanic Origin, in Current and Constant (2006) Dollars: 1980–2006

Year	Median income in current dollars					Median income in constant (2006) dollars				
	All house-holds [1]	White [2]	Black [3]	Asian, Pacific Islander [4]	His-panic [5]	All house-holds [1]	White [2]	Black [3]	Asian, Pacific Islander [4]	His-panic [5]
1980	17,710	18,684	10,764	(NA)	13,651	41,258	43,527	25,076	(NA)	31,802
1990	29,943	31,231	18,676	38,450	22,330	44,778	46,705	27,929	57,500	33,394
1995 [6]	34,076	35,766	22,393	40,614	22,860	44,764	46,985	29,417	53,353	30,030
1998	38,885	40,912	25,351	46,637	28,330	48,034	50,538	31,316	57,610	34,996
1999 [7]	40,696	42,325	27,910	50,960	30,746	49,244	51,215	33,773	61,664	37,204
2000 [8]	41,990	43,916	29,667	55,757	33,168	49,163	51,418	34,735	65,281	38,834
2001	42,228	44,517	29,470	53,635	33,565	48,091	50,698	33,562	61,082	38,225
2002 [9]	42,409	45,086	29,026	52,020	33,103	47,530	50,530	32,531	58,980	37,100
2003	43,318	45,631	29,645	55,699	32,997	47,488	50,023	32,499	61,061	36,173
2004 [10]	44,334	46,658	30,095	57,504	34,271	47,323	49,803	32,124	61,380	36,581
2005	46,326	48,554	30,858	61,094	35,967	47,845	50,146	31,870	63,097	37,146
2006	48,201	50,673	31,969	64,238	37,781	48,201	50,673	31,969	64,238	37,781

NA Not available. [1] Includes other races not shown separately. [2] Beginning with 2002, data represent White alone, which refers to people who reported White and did not report any other race category. [3] Beginning with 2002, data represent Black alone, which refers to people who reported Black and did not report any other race category. [4] Beginning with 2002, data represent Asian alone, which refers to people who reported Asian and did not report any other race category. [5] People of Hispanic origin may be of any race. [6] Data reflect full implementation of the 1990 census-based sample design and metropolitan definitions, 7,000 household sample reduction, and revised race edits. [7] Implementation of Census 2000-based population controls. [8] Implementation of a 28,000 household sample expansion. [9] See footnote 3, Table 668. [10] Data have been revised to reflect a correction to the weights in the 2005 ASEC.

SOURCE: U.S. CENSUS BUREAU, CURRENT POPULATION REPORTS, P60–233; AND INTERNET SITES <HTTP://WWW.CENSUS .GOV/PROD/2007PUBS/P60-233.PDF>(RELEASED AUGUST 2007) AND <HTTP://WWW.CENSUS.GOV/HHES/WWW/INCOME/ HISTINC/H05.HTML>.

one-stop shop for those looking for the latest turn of the screw on some of the economic statistics scattered on other, less-than-user-friendly Web sites maintained by the Feds."[55]

Forbes magazine named EconomicIndicators.gov "Best of the Web," explaining that "this site simply links to the relevant department's Web site. This might not seem like a big deal, but doing it yourself—say, trying to find retail sales data on the Census Bureau's site—is such an exercise in futility that it will convince you why this portal is necessary."[56]

No wonder the Bush administration wanted to shut this site down. It provided the American people with information about the state of the U.S. economy.

On February 13, 2008, Think Progress reported that the Bush administration would shut down EconomicIndicators due to "bud-getary restraints." Sure enough, visitors to the Web site could read

FIGURE 21

People Below Poverty Level and Below 125 Percent of Poverty Level by Race and Hispanic Origin: 1980 to 2006

[(29,272 represents 29,272,000.) People as of March of the following year. Based on Current Population Survey, Annual Social and Economic Supplement (ASEC); See text, Section 1, and Appendix III. For data collection changes over time, see <http://www.census.gov/hhes/www/income/histinc/hstchg.html>]

Year	Number below poverty level (1,000)					Percent below poverty level					Below 125 percent of poverty level	
	All races[1]	White[2]	Black[3]	Asian and Pacific Islander[4]	Hispanic[5]	All races[1]	White[2]	Black[3]	Asian and Pacific Islander[4]	Hispanic[5]	Number (1,000)	Percent of total population
1980....	29,272	19,699	8,579	(NA)	3,491	13.0	10.2	32.5	(NA)	25.7	40,658	18.1
1985....	33,064	22,860	8,926	(NA)	5,236	14.0	11.4	31.3	(NA)	29.0	44,166	18.7
1986....	32,370	22,183	8,983	(NA)	5,117	13.6	11.0	31.1	(NA)	27.3	43,486	18.2
1987[6]..	32,221	21,195	9,520	1,021	5,422	13.4	10.4	32.4	16.1	28.0	43,032	17.9
1988....	31,745	20,715	9,356	1,117	5,357	13.0	10.1	31.3	17.3	26.7	42,551	17.5
1989....	31,528	20,785	9,302	939	5,430	12.8	10.0	30.7	14.1	26.2	42,653	17.3
1990....	33,585	22,326	9,837	858	6,006	13.5	10.7	31.9	12.2	28.1	44,837	18.0
1991[7]..	35,708	23,747	10,242	996	6,339	14.2	11.3	32.7	13.8	28.7	47,527	18.9
1992[7]..	38,014	25,259	10,827	985	7,592	14.8	11.9	33.4	12.7	29.6	50,592	19.7
1993[8]..	39,265	26,226	10,877	1,134	8,126	15.1	12.2	33.1	15.3	30.6	51,801	20.0
1994....	38,059	25,379	10,196	974	8,416	14.5	11.7	30.6	14.6	30.7	50,401	19.3
1995....	36,425	24,423	9,872	1,411	8,574	13.8	11.2	29.3	14.6	30.3	48,761	18.5
1996....	36,529	24,650	9,694	1,454	8,697	13.7	11.2	28.4	14.5	29.4	49,310	18.5
1997....	35,574	24,396	9,116	1,468	8,308	13.3	11.0	26.5	14.0	27.1	47,853	17.8
1998....	34,476	23,454	9,091	1,360	8,070	12.7	10.5	26.1	12.5	25.6	46,036	17.0
1999[9]..	32,791	22,169	8,441	1,285	7,876	11.9	9.8	23.6	10.7	22.7	45,030	16.3
2000[10]..	31,581	21,645	7,982	1,258	7,747	11.3	9.5	22.5	9.9	21.5	43,612	15.6
2001[11]..	32,907	22,739	8,136	1,275	7,997	11.7	9.9	22.7	10.2	21.4	45,320	16.1
2002[11]..	34,570	23,466	8,602	1,161	8,555	12.1	10.2	24.1	10.1	21.8	47,084	16.5
2003....	35,861	24,272	8,781	1,401	9,051	12.5	10.5	24.4	11.8	22.5	48,687	16.9
2004[12]..	37,040	25,327	9,014	1,201	9,122	12.7	10.8	24.7	9.8	21.9	49,693	17.1
2005....	36,950	24,872	9,168	1,402	9,368	12.6	10.6	24.9	11.1	21.8	49,327	16.8
2006....	36,460	24,416	9,048	1,353	9,243	12.3	10.3	24.3	10.3	20.6	49,688	16.8

NA Not available. [1]Includes other races not shown separately. [2]Beginning 2002, data represent White alone, which refers to people who reported White and did not report any other race category. [3]Beginning 2002, data represent Black alone, which refers to people who reported Black and did not report any other race category. [4]Beginning 2002, data represent Asian alone, which refers to people who reported Asian and did not report any other race category. [5]People of Hispanic origin may be of any race. [6]Implementation of a new March CPS processing system. [7]Implementation of 1990 census population controls. [8]The March 1994 income supplement was revised to allow for the coding of different income amounts on selected questionnaire items. Limits either increased or decreased in the following categories: earnings increased to $999,999; social security increased to $49,999; supplemental security income and public assistance increased to $24,999; veterans' benefits increased to $99,999; child support and alimony decreased to $49,999. [9]Implementation of Census 2000-based population controls. [10]Implementation of sample expansion by 28,000 households. [11]Beginning with the 2003 Current Population Survey (CPS), the questionnaire allowed respondents to choose more than one race. For 2002 and later, data represent persons who selected this race group only and exclude persons reporting more than one race. The CPS in prior years allowed respondents to report only one race group. [12]Data have been revised to reflect a correction to the weights in the 2005 ASEC.

SOURCE: U.S. CENSUS BUREAU, CURRENT POPULATION REPORTS, P60–233; AND INTERNET SITES <HTTP://WWW.CENSUS .GOV/PROD/2007PUBS/P60–233.PDF> (RELEASED AUGUST 2007) AND <HTTP://WWW.CENSUS.GOV/HHES/WWW/POVERTY/ HISTPOV/PERINDEX.HTML>.

that it would stop operating beginning March 1, 2008.[57] Of course, because it's Bush, they weren't really just shutting it down. Bush and his greedy cronies just wanted to start charging anyone who wanted the data a fee.

Then Senator Chuck Schumer was on the case. He said, somewhat pointedly, "On the brink of a possible recession, the Bush

FIGURE 22

Children Below Poverty Level by Race and Hispanic Origin: 1980 to 2006

[11,114 represents 11,114,000. **Persons as of March of the following year.** Covers only related children in families under 18 years old. Based on Current Population Survey; see text, this section and Section 1, and Appendix III. For data collection changes over time, see <http://www.census.gov/hhes/www/income/histinc/hstchg.html>]

Year	Number below poverty level (1,000)					Percent below poverty level				
	All races [1]	White [2]	Black [3]	Asian and Pacific Islander [4]	His-panic [5]	All races [1]	White [2]	Black [3]	Asian and Pacific Islander [4]	His-panic [5]
1980	11,114	6,817	3,906	(NA)	1,718	17.9	13.4	42.1	(NA)	33.0
1985 [6]	12,483	7,838	4,057	(NA)	2,512	20.1	15.6	43.1	(NA)	39.6
1987 [6]	12,275	7,398	4,234	432	2,606	19.7	14.7	44.4	22.7	38.9
1988	11,935	7,095	4,148	458	2,576	19.0	14.0	42.8	23.5	37.3
1989	12,001	7,164	4,257	368	2,496	19.0	14.1	43.2	18.9	35.5
1990	12,715	7,696	4,412	356	2,750	19.9	15.1	44.2	17.0	37.7
1991 [7]	13,658	8,316	4,637	348	2,977	21.1	16.1	45.6	17.1	39.8
1992 [7]	14,521	8,752	5,015	352	3,440	21.6	16.5	46.3	16.0	39.0
1993 [8]	14,961	9,123	5,030	358	3,666	22.0	17.0	45.9	17.6	39.9
1994	14,610	8,826	4,787	308	3,956	21.2	16.3	43.3	17.9	41.1
1995	13,999	8,474	4,644	532	3,938	20.2	15.5	41.5	18.6	39.3
1996	13,764	8,488	4,411	553	4,090	19.8	15.5	39.5	19.1	39.9
1997	13,422	8,441	4,116	608	3,865	19.2	15.4	36.8	19.9	36.4
1998	12,845	7,935	4,073	542	3,670	18.3	14.4	36.4	17.5	33.6
1999 [9]	11,678	7,194	3,698	367	3,561	16.6	13.1	32.8	11.5	30.0
2000 [10] . . .	11,005	6,834	3,495	407	3,342	15.6	12.4	30.9	12.5	27.6
2001	11,175	7,086	3,423	353	3,433	15.8	12.8	30.0	11.1	27.4
2002 [11] . . .	11,646	7,203	3,570	302	3,653	16.3	13.1	32.1	11.4	28.2
2003	12,340	7,624	3,750	331	3,982	17.2	13.9	33.6	12.1	29.5
2004 [12] . . .	12,473	7,876	3,702	265	3,985	17.3	14.3	33.4	9.4	28.6
2005	12,335	7,652	3,743	312	3,077	17.1	13.9	34.2	11.0	27.7
2006	12,299	7,522	3,690	351	3,959	16.9	13.6	33.0	12.0	26.6

NA Not available. [1]Includes other races not shown separately. [2]Beginning 2002, data represent White alone, which refers to people who reported White and did not report any other race category. [3]Beginning 2002, data represent Black alone, which refers to people who reported Black and did not report any other race category. [4]Beginning 2002, data represent Asian alone, which refers to people who reported Asian and did not report any other race category. [5]People of Hispanic origin may be of any race. [6]Implementation of a new March CPS processing system. [7]Implementation of 1990 census population controls. [8]The March 1994 income supplement was revised to allow for the coding of different income amounts on selected questionnaire items. Limits either increased or decreased in the following categories: earnings increased to $999,999; social security increased to $49,999; supplemental security income and public assistance increased to $24,999; veterans' benefits increased to $99,999; child support and alimony decreased to $49,999. [9] Implementation of Census 2000-based population controls. [10]Implementation of sample expansion to 28,000 households. [11]Beginning with the 2003 Current Population Survey (CPS), the questionnaire allowed respondents to choose more than one race. For 2002 and later, data represent persons who selected this race group only and excludes persons reporting more than one race. The CPS in prior years allowed respondents to report only one race group. [12]Data have been revised to reflect a correction to the weights in the 2005 Annual Social and Economic Supplement (ASEC).

SOURCE: U.S. CENSUS BUREAU, CURRENT POPULATION REPORTS, P60–233; AND INTERNET SITES <HTTP://WWW.CENSUS .GOV/PROD/2007PUBS/P60–233.PDF>(RELEASED AUGUST 2007) AND <HTTP://WWW.CENSUS.GOV/HHES/WWW/POVERTY/ HISTPOV/HSTPOV3.HTML>.

Administration's decision to shut down the free flow of economic data boggles the mind. Wasteful government spending should be cut, but shutting down an award-winning website that gives Americans easy-to-use economic information during troubling economic times is penny-wise and pound-foolish."[58]

Only a week after the Bush administration said it would be

shutting down EconomicIndicators.gov, the *Wall Street Journal* reported that the administration had suddenly found room in the budget to continue the site.[59] The fact that it even tried to shut this site down is proof of just how aware it was that its economic record was nothing short of dismal.

Bush couldn't dodge his record. His efforts offer an instructive lesson to future presidents: it is not possible to sweep an entire presidency under the rug. His efforts to do so were, at the least, too little, too late. The mortgage crisis preceded an even deeper, more profound economic crisis as the stock market plummeted and took Americans' savings and retirement with it in the summer of 2008.

The secret's out: Democrats are better than Republicans on the economy. And guess what? I don't mean to shock anybody, but as it turns out, Bush distinguished himself as a particularly remarkable failure within the pantheon of Republican presidents who have wrought economic havoc. Many of Obama's most effective speeches have been about the economy, and for good reason. The American people are still feeling the devastating effects of the Bush administration and decades of cumulative conservative economic policy, and it's one of the biggest reasons for Democratic success in 2008—and why they're ready to keep electing Democrats.

IT'S NOT SUPPLY AND DEMAND

Throughout much of 2008, gas averaged somewhere north of $4 a gallon.

The Washington chatterrati and editorial boards insisted that basic supply and demand were to blame for increasingly high oil and gasoline prices.[60] Robert Samuelson, in his July 7 *Newsweek* column, mocked politicians for blaming speculators for the energy crisis. "A better explanation is basic supply and demand," he informed the reader.[61]

Call me a fool, but I'm suspicious of the claim that supply and demand is to blame for rocketing energy costs. I'd have to say that the lack of conservation policy, the weak dollar, out-of-control speculators, and the Bush administration's idiotic foreign policy might have had more to do with our soaring oil and gas prices.

For any who doubt that it's probably not just supply and demand, we have recent history as a guide. Let's take a trip back to the year of 2000, when California was entangled in its own serious energy crisis. Former Governor Gray Davis was being crucified by the media for stating that the state's deregulation of the energy companies had led to price manipulation. Davis called for price controls and more energy conservation measures.

Vice President Dick Cheney was involved with the Federal Energy Regulatory Commission (FERC) investigation into the debacle from the outset. From its inception, Cheney and the commission mocked claims of price manipulation. Cheney was as bold as to say, "Conservation may be a sign of personal virtue, but it is not a sufficient basis for a sound, comprehensive energy policy."[62] And you could guess, he was for more deregulation and increased drilling.

The chattering class was at it back then, too, and they were in agreement with Cheney. They balked at Davis's charges that Texas energy giants such as Enron would ever try to manipulate prices for their own corporate benefit.[63] The entire op-ed-writing, editorial-board-sitting, cocktail-party-attending, pipe-smoking, chin-scratching establishment lined up against Governor Davis, with the lone exception of now Nobel Prize winner Paul Krugman.

Lo and behold, it turns out former Governor Davis (and Krugman) were right. Three years after the crisis, Krugman got to write that "Most independent experts now believe that during 2000–2001, price manipulation by energy companies, mainly taking the form of 'economic withholding'—keeping capacity offline to drive up prices—added billions of dollars to California's electricity bills." That's also about the time that a March FERC report confirmed there had been "extensive manipulation" of energy prices.[64]

The 2000 crisis had everything to do with market manipulation and energy conservation. So count me as skeptical, Robert Samuelson and the rest of you, if I don't believe your supply-side shtick. I have an open mind with regard to whether the speculators and conservation and the weak dollar and our asinine foreign policy have everything to do with our recent energy crisis and the price of gas.

CHAPTER 11

Youth Voters

Since the late 1960s, the same chorus has been heard from election to election: The young don't care. They're disengaged. They're too wrapped up in their music, their favorite sports and their parties to take an interest in politics. Predicting that the young will vote in large numbers is like saying the Cubs will finally win the World Series. As it happens, the Cubs are doing well this season, and the evidence is overwhelming that this year the young really will vote in large numbers—and they just might tip the election."

—E.J. DIONNE, *THE WASHINGTON POST,*
JULY 25, 2008*

This year, 66% of those under age 30 voted for Barack Obama making the disparity between young voters and other age groups larger than in any presidential election since exit polling began in 1972.

—PEW, NOVEMBER 12, 2008[1]

Let's dispense with what we already know is going to be the Limbaugh-Wolfowitz-Horowitz-O'Reilly-Colbert answer to this chapter. It'll go something like this: being a Democrat is an indulgence of youth, because you haven't paid taxes and you haven't seen the

---

* The Cubs did, in fact, get swept out of the first round of the playoffs, but the youth vote did still make the difference in several key states in the 2008 election.

real world, but we love you, we forgive you, and we will embrace you into the pro-war, anti-environment, low-wage culture warriors when you inevitably age and wise up. They'll claim youth have always been more Democratic than older voters and point to the 1960s, to how many of them were liberals who later saw the light. But these turncoats are the exception, not the rule.

One thing they can't argue with is how diverse this generation is. Even Rush would have to admit that certain groups, regardless of age, tend to vote Democratic. Like African-Americans and Latinos, minus Cubans. That's something we can all pretty much agree on. (That's the only way I can understand how bad the Republicans are on minority issues—they know those votes are lost anyway.)

In light of this fact we can both agree on, there's more bad news for Republicans. The generation of young adults voting in 2008 is the most diverse in history. Back in 1972, almost nine in ten youth voters (87 percent) were white. By 2004, only 62 percent of youth said they were white. The percentage of the youth population that identifies as Latino more than doubled during that time, from 5 to 12 percent.[2] The trends in voting among these diverse groups favor the Democrats.

Now we'll get to the more controversial part. That's when we have to ask these folks telling us that being a Democrat is a symptom of being young, is voting behavior really that flexible? Do people just switch parties, stop giving a damn about schools and civil liberties, as soon as they pull out their checkbook to pay taxes?

In a word, no. This theory of voter behavior has about as much supporting evidence as creationism. People have actually gone out and researched these things. All these right-wing people are dead-ass wrong. Allow me to steer you toward a word that drives them all crazy: science.

The research is on our side. Psychology says that people's political attitudes stabilize as they age. Once people reach their thirties, their political ideology is more or less set.[3] Political scientists studying trends and patterns and so on concluded that "It is apparent . . . that identification with political parties, once established, is an attachment which is not easily changed."[4] There's also the fact that the National Election Studies in the 1950s and 1970s agreed that "Party identification was the most stable attitude measured . . . indeed almost perfectly stable."[5] Studies in the 1990s confirmed these findings, showing that once voters' party identification is set, it tends to stick.[6]

Another item of evidence for their consideration is the fact that the gap in party identification among young people has rarely been so dramatic as in 2008. To revisit a point made in an earlier chapter, the fact is, Democrats had a 19-point advantage among young voters. In 2004, the Democrats had only a 2-point advantage in party identification.[7] In any other year, Republicans might be able to dismiss their disadvantage among young voters with the oft-repeated claim that youth simply tend to be more liberal than their parents, but this year they've got 19 points to explain away.

What's worse news for the Republicans is the fact that youth didn't just vote for Obama last year—they volunteered, knocked on doors, distributed pamphlets, and drove other people to the polls. That's the type of investment in a candidate and party that cements political leanings. To go back to Curtis Gans of American University, "the more important contribution of the college-educated young was in providing the sinew for Obama's extensive grassroots organization which was, in part, responsible for the large increase in Democratic turnout."[8] This spring 75 percent of youth are following the Obama administration and politics writ large closely or very closely.[9]

There's a window in which voters' major political attitudes form, and for this youngest voting generation, that window was the George W. Bush administration. Bush's greatest contribution to the country may have been making sure that there's no chance any Republican will be elected again while this bloc of voters has any say. One of these political scientists studying young voters wrote: "All the research done on the dramatic Democratic realignment of the 1930s shows that the key was young voters, coming of age as the Depression hit, influenced deeply by the contrast between Hoover and Roosevelt . . . those young voters became lifelong Democrats."[10] Asked how they were likely to vote in 2010, in the midterm elections, young voters were 53 to 31 percent in favor of a Democratic candidate over a Republican.[11]

The Bush administration brought us the war in Iraq, the chaos after Katrina, pervasive corruption, and a recession. Those were the events that defined the Republican Party for these young people. The fact that youth are overwhelmingly Democratic is no surprise. It's more surprising to me that there are any young people out there who are Republicans. For their part, the Republicans know they're in trouble, and they're sweating the youth vote. They want it back.

Now that I've gone through the psychologists' and political scientists' opinions, let me give my Carville commonsense take on the youth vote. In television terms, the new "key demographic" is younger people. All advertisers really give a shit about these days are those under forty-nine years old. It's this younger demographic in particular that they're obsessed with. Advertising rates and as a result network profitability are almost exclusively driven by the ability of a show to attract younger viewers. Are these advertisers idiots? Or is there actually a reason behind this?

I would suggest that there's a reason behind it. Older people are already set in their purchasing habits and, to be depressingly frank, they've got less time left to purchase. Young voters, to be equally brutally frank, can still be influenced, and it doesn't take an actuary to figure out that a twenty-five-year-old is likely going to vote in more elections in the future than a sixty-five-year-old.

We can think of the choice between parties in economic terms. Let's say you want to buy into a company, so you commission a study to see who is buying that company's product and what the consumer base would mean for long-term growth for that company. That's the type of cold, hard decision that people have to make every day. Well, look at the Republicans. The prime consumers of their product, or their ideology, belong to shrinking demographics, which is to say that, as a company, the Republican Party is headed for bankruptcy. Republicans' consumers, or supporters, are rapidly shrinking as a market share, leaving the Republicans without anyone to buy what we'll politely call "products" here.

As simple as this may sound to you, dear reader, you never can be too simple on the chance that some right-winger might pick this book up and read it. These many paragraphs are a laborious way to get to the central point, and that is simply this: the biggest political story unfolding in U.S. politics today is the ongoing collapse of the Republican Party among young voters.

The negative events and policies Republicans have been responsible for over the last eight years were the formative experiences today's youth cite as the equivalent of JFK's assassination in mine: the war in Iraq, the 2000 election in Florida, and Hurricane Katrina. They've given youth, as Obama would say, a sense of the urgency of now.

Youth Issues

To win young people, you have to be on the right side of three things: the economy; the war in Iraq; and the environment. The economy is one of young people's top concerns.[12] That's not exactly what we might call shocking. Young people looking for jobs can't find them. In the summer of 2008, this country had the highest teenage unemployment rate it's had in sixteen years—20.3 percent.[13] Moving from teenagers to all young people, that's usually anyone eighteen to twenty-nine, it's just one in three who thinks they've got a chance at a good job.[14] That's frightening.

Now on to the environment. This youngest generation of voters will inherit every one of our current environmental problems magnified by a thousand unless we do something drastic now. Say you're twenty-four. You have to inhabit the planet, on optimistic average, for another sixty years or so. So, logically, you're going to tend to be more concerned with the environment, global warming, and energy independence than most voters in other age groups. You have a bigger stake in it than an older person.

Being concerned about global warming is not, as the right-wing pontificators would claim, an indulgence of youth or a perceived problem that's being drilled into your head by a bunch of pinko left-wing college professors, nutty columnists, and talking heads. You're a rational person. You know it's getting hot. You know it from empirical evidence, and you know it because, well, it's getting hotter. If you're twenty-four, you know it's hotter now than it was when you were fourteen.

So, do young people believe that conservation is merely a personal virtue, as Dick Cheney declared so famously?[15] Do they believe that it's a good idea, as President Bush does, to allow coal companies to blow the tops off mountains and let the refuse slide down into the valley? (God knows one thing we have too many of in the United States is mountaintops. We could all do with fewer of those.) No, in short, young people believe conservation is necessary, not optional, and they want to protect the environment—not trade it in for a quick buck.

And lest I forget, there's another issue, besides the Bush economic and energy policies crippling our young people, that will continue competing for their attention in 2009. That would be the war in Iraq. It's mostly young people dying in Iraq and Afghanistan, and it's young people who would be drafted pretty soon if we "stay the course" with the current rate of recruitment and retention. It's also young people who are going to inherit the ravaged domestic economy and international relations nightmare that the Republicans have created with the invasion of Iraq. The amount approved to date for spending in Iraq as I write could have paid for scholarships for more than 101 million Americans to go to college for a year.[16]

The economy, the environment, and Iraq: check, check, and check. The Democrats are on the right side of all these issues that are going to matter to youth. But it's not enough just to be right in 2008. Democrats have to make sure that youth's identification with the Democratic Party remains stable throughout their lives. That means Democrats can't just be the alternative to Brand R—or just get out the vote in 2008—we have to be a strong, appealing Brand D to solidify the gains we've made in this generation. Keep reading to The Real Deal for a "how-to" on building a strong Brand D.

CHAPTER 12

Accountability, Not Reform

The job Obama faces seems obvious. We've got sinking cities, collapsing bridges, soldiers in maggot-infested hospitals, a broken army, exploding numbers of uninsured Americans, melting polar caps—you name it. There's hardly a facet of life in America or the world that doesn't demand some quick, decisive action on the part of the U.S. government.

That's why on Election Night, November 4, 2008, masses of people were out in the streets cheering all over the world. On January 20, 2009, the nation and the world breathed a collective sigh of relief upon the realization that the U.S. government was ready to take action pronto. It was the moment we'd all been waiting for.

But hold on, Kemosabe, not so fast.

There's one little, minor problem that we have to deal with first: people no longer trust not just the Republicans but this government to do anything. George W. Bush's monumental conservative achievement is that he has undermined Americans' faith in their own government.

In May 2008, as the economic crisis was taking hold, just 37 percent of people, fewer than four in ten, felt favorably toward the federal government. In January 2007, as many people liked the government (45 percent) as disliked it (46 percent). Flash back a few years to December 2002, early in Bush's first term, when almost two thirds of people (64 percent) felt favorably toward government and fewer than three in ten (27 percent) took issue with it. That's the Bush effect.

I can predict a few ways the Bush administration could try to excuse this retroactively. Let's address the big one right now—this isn't a broad antigovernment attitude or a social trend that's been occurring independently of the Bush administration. People still like their state and local governments. It's six in ten people who hold a "favorable" view of their state government and more than six in ten (63 percent) who like their local government. Those numbers have held steady since 2002.[1]

So now comes the two-part question of the moment. What do we do about this, and where does this fit into the much-dreaded litany—or, as I would prefer to call it, the narrative—of the Democratic Party?

It's time to make reform the highest priority of the Democratic agenda. You're thinking, if you're still with me here, what are you talking about, James? How many times have we had the same discussion? I hear it over and over: "Nobody in my district cares about reform." Everyone who comes to Washington says no more business as usual, but there's only one way to do business in Washington.

They'll tell you that any issues poll ranks almost everything higher than "reform." The war in Iraq, health care, Social Security, stagnant wages, and nuclear proliferation are all higher priorities. Reform appeals only to a bunch of rich, suburban women in Montgomery County, Maryland, and it has nothing to do with the union halls and church basements where the heart and soul of the American Democratic Party resides. The average Democrat out in the country never brings up any of these issues in any town hall meeting.

All of the congressmen and women say pushing reform is a waste of time. In Latin, it's just *appesumatum editorialisma*. It's an overused word that folks just toss around. Every huckster that's ever tried to scam the government for anything has done so under the guise of reform.

Republicans love to "reform" things. They "reformed" Medicare on behalf of big drug companies, and they tried to "reform" education and "reform" Social Security. "Reform," in the literal sense, is exactly the right word. Republicans love to take apart government programs and re-form them so that they more closely resemble something that benefits corporations and Republican interests.

So, okay, you've won. To hell with the word "reform." You're right. I don't want reform. I want accountability. It has the added advantage of sounding responsible, even conservative. It's a solid word with concrete policy implications.

Republicans will hate it because it would make government the thing that they fear most, accountable to the people. It'd be harder to trash government then. And if government were accountable, Republicans wouldn't be able to point to partisan failures as proof of government failure.

So, my dear friends, I am suggesting that we remember to place accountability at the very center of the Democratic narrative going forward, at every level. It's the simplest thing in the world. Understand that if you are the party of government action, if you think that the federal government has been and can be a positive force in American life, then you have to be for accountability.

If you think that government is the root of evil and the creator of problems, then you're anti-accountability—you don't want people to trust the government, and you delight in stories of government incompetence. Your dream day starts out reading the newspaper about a broken levee, because that just proves to you that government can't do anything. You can use that as an example of why we don't need environmental regulations, why we don't need safety laws, why we don't need National Parks, publicly funded museums, or even public schools. Because if government can't build a levee, what can it do? (Of course it was a private contractor that build the levee, but that doesn't fit their narrative, so let's let that go.)

People have lost faith in government. It's a fact. We Democrats cannot do what we all too often do and blame people instead of addressing their real concerns. It's up to us to put accountability front and center.

Let's go back to Basic Communication 101. What constitutes a narrative? It is simply this: every book ever written, every movie ever made, every story ever told has a basic construct: setup, conflict, and resolution. That's the way that the human mind absorbs information. There is no other way to communicate. The human mind does not absorb information through a litany. Litanies are boring and meaningless, and they lead to defeat in elections.

It's like I said before, in *Take It Back* and a thousand other places: Democrats need a narrative. I'm sick of trying to find new ways to say it, and even more sick of having a wealth of examples of Democratic failure to draw from, so I'm going to repeat myself unapologetically here:

- "By being too timid or too weak or too confused, Democrats have allowed Republicans to run amok. Most important, Democrats have not clearly and courageously stated what they stand for and what they stand against."
- "Democrats have failed at the basics: defining their message, attacking their opponents, defending their leaders, inspiring their voters."
- "It's not that people know what we stand for and disagree; it's that they have no idea what we stand for, and so they think we're too weak to lead."[2]

Think of *The Godfather*. Setup: You meet everyone in the family and community. They eat pasta and drink wine and run a crime syndicate. Some you like, some you don't. Someone comes in and shoots the Godfather. The rest of the time there's a conflict between the Corleones and the Tattaglias. Then Michael comes in and blows all of their asses away. There's your resolution.

In every movie, every book, every everything, there's setup, conflict, then resolution. That's how it goes every time.

When my daughters were little, they'd bring me a Winnie-the-Pooh book, and, like a good father, I'd read it to them. It was always the same deal. Winnie lost the honey, and Piglet and Tigger were always confused and didn't know what to do. Then they brought in

Christopher Robin, and he found it for them. That's what it was. You got the setup, you liked all the characters in the Hundred Acre Woods, you were rooting for them when there was a problem, and you were delighted and relieved when Christopher Robin came in and saved everyone at the end.

If you get a Ph.D. in classics from Oxford and you read the *Iliad*, which I never have, it's going to be the same basic structure. It doesn't change.

So there's a nifty narrative here, that America was a nation that was making some progress. We were respected around the world. We were getting things done. And then the Bush administration came in and government fell apart. Now we have to make government accountable to the people, and once we've done that, we can begin to accomplish the things we have always dreamed of.

America was reducing poverty, running surpluses, and building its reputation around the world. Then comes the conflict. The bad guys ride into town—and I'll let you figure out who the bad guys are in this scenario—to destroy progress, accountability, reputation, and all sense of responsibility. Last comes the resolution. A posse of good folks led by President Obama rides into town, runs the bad guys out, says we're going to restore the faith of the people. Schoolmarms, preachers, teachers, and storekeepers are happy again. Therein lies the simplicity of the accountability message.

So let's apply our newfound knowledge of narrative. Let's set about crafting a message that wraps up accountability and policies. Let's get a Real Deal. Turn the page, loyal reader.

CHAPTER 13

The Real Deal

The scene is lunch at the Palm. Second-from-rear booth on the north side. Half-drunk bourbons and iced teas and red wine glasses and other evidence of long and protracted conversation. It's a cast of the usual suspects: Begala, Carville, a Senate chief of staff or two, a left-of-center commentator, a columnist, and a few other bloviators. Espressos and lattes sit in front of the diners, steaming slightly.

The journalist pauses and says, somewhat profoundly, as journalists tend to try to do, "You've got the House, the Senate, and the White House. So, what's the Big Idea?" Everyone nods thoughtfully. Begala, being a constant notetaker, whips out pad and pen.

The sound now? Thundering silence.

At the moment that this book is being sent to print, President Obama is facing a number of distractions that are substantially hindering his attempts to make progress on the ideas and policies he was elected to implement. If Obama is going to try to reform and repair policy in a big way, he's going to need an umbrella—a hook, an explanation, a reason, whatever you want to call it. What he lacks, what we as a party lack, is not ideas but a hook for these ideas. There's got to be a coherent framework for his proposals. Our suggestion is to call it the Real Deal. It's time for President Obama to tell Republicans to get real about this situation and offer Americans a Real Deal.

Americans need and deserve a Real Deal. The most obvious and overwhelming truth about the Bush years—also known as the regrettable post-Clinton, pre-Obama period—is that reality and policy making were completely divorced. The hallmark of the Bush-Cheney policy process was ideologically driven irrationality. The genesis of every piece of Bush-Cheney policy over eight years was ideological. Science, fiscal policy, foreign policy, health care policy—you name it—was guided by conservative and far-right ideologues and sycophants of the most despicable persuasion.

Enter Obama. Americans are sick of policy making based in ideology. The new president is attempting to introduce some sort of rational, reality-based considerations into politics, and, again, I think he should call it the Real Deal. I can hear him delivering the line: "It's time for America to get real." After eight years of weathering Bush policies totally detached from reality, from a war to economic policies that ushered in economic catastrophe, that's an explanation that people understand.

What Obama's faced with is a set of old issues that are newly urgent. We've been tossing national health insurance around since the 1940s with Truman. Nixon, of all people, championed environmental policy thirty years ago. What we need is a new Big Idea to place them in a framework that we can all relate to and understand.

Taking a step back, what *is* a Big Idea?

There have been only two good Big Ideas in the forty years since LBJ brought in the Great Society. They were both conservative. That would be supply-side economics and neoconservatism. They were new, bold, easy to explain, and profoundly stupid.

Supply-side economics and neoconservatism have had a tremendous impact on the political landscape and thought. One could even call them radical, transformational, paradigmatic, sweeping ideas. After all, there's nothing more radical than the idea that you could invade a country without a history of unity, build a parliament and stock exchange, and manufacture a beacon of liberal democracy that would be a friend to us, a supporter of Israel, and a fine, upstanding member of the world community.

You could argue, though you'd lose, that the 1980s and 1990s had a few other good Big Ideas. Compassionate conservatism, perhaps. But that was more a slogan than a Big Idea. That same could probably be said of Obama's rallying cries of "Yes we can" and "Change we can believe in." (A slogan is a necessary but not sufficient component of a Big Idea.) There were no truly new policies behind "compassionate conservatism," just the same old schtick. Not like Great Society's Medicare or Medicaid. Those were truly stunning policy innovations.

The obvious candidate of the past few years for status of Big Idea is the "War on Terror." It's certainly a rallying cry. Like "neoconservatism" and "supply-side economics," it's now part of the American political vocabulary—and like both, it's been exposed as seriously strategically flawed. Now the Bush administration has pulled back from calling it a "War on Terror" to something a bit more negotiable—"a global struggle against extremism" or some such thing. The "War on Terror" is a good example of how so many ideas that appear to be bold and new—and good—at a certain point in time don't stand up to scrutiny that well.

I don't know if the "War on Terror" is a Big Idea, but I don't think so. A Big Idea is a full set of policies that applies to social and economic conditions—it's something sweeping like the Square Deal, the Fair Deal, the New Deal, neoconservatism, or supply-side economics, as I said earlier.

The outcome of the two Big Ideas I've nominated, supply-side economics and neoconservatism, is that we're primed for a Democratic Big Idea. Just look at Jonathan Chait's book, *The Big Con*, for a stunningly helpful exposé on just how much of an absurdity these conservative creations were from conception to execution, and just how much damage they've done. He calls the conservatives who support these ideas deranged. All I can say is, "Hello, $5.5 trillion surplus; goodbye, $5.5 trillion surplus."

So the scene is set for Obama to sweep in with a new Big Idea. The failure of the Republicans' Big Ideas helped lay the groundwork for Democratic successes. Given the circumstances of the country and Obama's victory, Obama is perfectly positioned to ex-

ecute whatever this hypothetical next Democratic Big Idea is. He's
got a wide, deep base and, to put it modestly, unusually good communications skills and a public unusually receptive to large-picture
solutions. Anyone interested in solutions can't help but be struck
by a sense of optimism at Obama's ability to get things done. Having been a supporter of his opponent, I cannot help but say that his
initial decisions have been not just reassuring but inspiring.

What next?

On the Democratic side, we feel compelled to debate and chatter and write op-eds and talk about the search for the new Big Idea.
We review our party history compulsively, sifting through and
searching for a hint. So let's do some of that.

Think back to the first really great Big Idea, the one that comes
to mind any time anyone says, "Big Idea." That's the New Deal.
Teddy may have introduced the Square Deal three decades before,
but it was Franklin's New Deal in 1932 that had the greatest impact. He said, in 1932 in Chicago, Illinois, as he presented the New
Deal:

> I pledge you, I pledge myself, to a new deal for the American
> people. Let us all here assembled constitute ourselves prophets
> of a new order of competence and of courage. This is more than
> a political campaign; it is a call to arms. Give me your help, not
> to win votes alone, but to win in this crusade to restore America
> to its own people.

Roosevelt's New Deal language was eloquent, thoughtful, and
persuasive—and it was sloganeering at its best. There's nothing at
all new there.

What about Kennedy? Asked to identify the height of Democratic oratory in this century, to come up with one line from any
address since World War II, Americans will tell you it was JFK's
"ask not what your country can do for you—ask what you can do
for your country." It's the same message. Roosevelt said it was "a
call to arms" and asked for all Americans' help. Kennedy retooled
it subtly, but it's essentially the same message.

If the people who covered the 2008 campaign were covering Roosevelt's speech in 1932 or even Kennedy's inaugural address, they'd call it empty rhetoric. There was no five-point plan, no immediate enumeration of policy proposals forthcoming. The *Washington Post* editorial board would have called FDR's rhetoric "detached from reality."

It may be that Americans are too cynical for Big Ideas now, that we're just not in the market for them or we're too worried about the stock market. But the bigger problem is, there is no new Big Idea—there never has been.

Every Big Idea was just a new way of presenting old ideas with a few twists. The New Deal brought us new forms of social spending through Social Security, for example, while the Great Society created Medicare and Medicaid. In the case of supply-side economics, the new policy was (newly justified) tax cuts for the wealthy. So, really, there's just new packaging, new strategy, and better narratives.

So, then, you might think, what Obama should really be after is a partywide Manhattan Project. That's the 1992 edition, not 1941. The Manhattan Project, for my younger or less political audience, was the undertaking of reintroducing Bill Clinton to the electorate after the disastrous primary of 1992, so called because we got the green light for our idea while in Manhattan.

The election is over. Democrats have majorities in the House and Senate, and we have the White House. What is the next Democratic Big Idea? Where's the post-2008 matchbook? (A Big Idea, readers, is an idea so potently, powerfully, obviously resonant it can be summarized on the back of a matchbook.) There's no shortage of people out there with ideas about what the Big Idea ought to be.

Let's go through the clearly defined elements of the next Democratic Big Idea and the priorities of the Obama administration.

First and foremost, the environment. There's no real dissent among the non-lobotomized world that (a) global warming is real and proven; (b) human behavior contributes significantly; and

(c) something has to be done, and done pronto. It might take the form of a massive project to achieve energy independence, and it's certainly going to involve policies and regulations reducing reliance on carbon, addressing global warming, and working to ease the effects already emerging.

A second and related component of the next Democratic platform has to be energy independence. Newt Gingrich and these Republicans have this idea they're really big on: they think we can drill our way to cheaper gas prices and energy independence. Here's my question for them: of the proven oil reserves, what percentage are in the United States? What worldwide reserves are left?

We can't drill our way to energy independence. Even if we drilled ANWR, destroying a pristine, gorgeous wildlife reserve to feed this nasty energy habit, it wouldn't do a thing to lower the price of gas. Not only that, it'd take ten years just to get some kind of usable oil out of Alaska, no matter what Sarah Palin says. Same thing for offshore drilling in Florida and California.

The worldwide picture isn't much better. The percentage of our oil supply coming from the Persian Gulf in 1961 was 18 percent. Today, it's 17 percent. Over forty-six years, we haven't managed to maintain a decrease in our reliance on Persian Gulf oil by more than a percentage point.

Imagine a terrible, terrible global event. A natural disaster or a (new) war. If we lost Persian Gulf and South American suppliers simultaneously, we'd lose 36 percent of our oil supply. We'd suddenly find ourselves relying on Mexico, Canada, Norway, and Great Britain for the majority of our oil imports.

Say Mexico falls prey to the same instabilities already plaguing its Spanish-speaking neighbors to the south in our hypothetical situation. That cuts us to 52 percent, or about half, of our previous oil supply. Bottom line: We can't continue to rely on some of the most unstable or unpredictable countries in the world for our energy supply.

If all the voters agree that something is good, that makes it good

politics. If all the experts agree that something is good, that generally makes it good policy. If something is good politics and good
policy, why aren't we running like crazy with it? Energy independence, energy conservation, alternative energy, you name it—
these ideas win. And when I say it's good politics, I mean, it's really
good politics. (Or, as the Web site would say, it's really clear that
it's really good politics.)

For example, in an ABC News/*Washington Post* poll, 63 percent
of people said that the government should offer tax breaks to corporations as incentives to develop alternative energy. Only 32 percent said that government should leave the development of
alternative energy to the marketplace.[1] (I'd bet that after the dramatic failures of the marketplace over the last year, even fewer
would be willing to leave anything to the market today.)

Then there's the economy. After these last few years of stagnant
and declining incomes, second jobs, record foreclosures, and disappearing retirements, the next Big Idea will also have to reshape
economic policy in a few big ways—especially tax policy. That includes eliminating or lessening the burden of payroll tax to allevi-
ate income inequality and examining tax breaks—including the
capital gains tax.

There couldn't have been anything wackier in 2001 than passing
a tax cut for rich people or eliminating the Paris Hilton estate tax.
It's stunning that this administration blew a $5.5 trillion surplus on
5 percent of the American people while we have a rapidly rising
problem of income inequality and a panoply of unmet fiscal needs.

We're also going to have to take on universal health insurance
in some form. The final product will likely be some cocktail of new
requirements for businesses and employers, subsidies, and tax
breaks to make insurance more affordable.

An equally apparent reality is that Obama will have to redress
problems with social programs. That means fixing Social Security. It's going to require some intervention. Do the math. It doesn't
work. I wish it did. (Privatization also doesn't work, for the record.)

Obama will also have to make education a priority. Higher education is more important than ever before to opportunity and earn-

ings. So we'll need to talk about ways to rebuild our public schools and make college more affordable. And we'll need to establish a new form of civic education and improve access to information and technology. Broadband in every house could make information available freely and make our society even more, and even more truly, democratic.

Then there's the global picture. That pesky matter of multilateral foreign policy. Obama and Biden will need to retool the U.S. approach to international organizations and treaties and will have to revise foreign aid restrictions and priorities. It's a Jeffrey Sachs world out there. There's malaria, HIV/AIDS, and widespread abject poverty.

And if the environment is the headliner, the closer of any Democratic Big Idea—its foundation and bedrock—has to be some form of anticorruption initiative. The last Democratic lobbying reform bill Bush had to sign was a great start, and Obama began by championing strong, even harsh, policies on lobbying. But keeping an eye on the prize, anticorruption has been a staple of every Big Idea since the first Roosevelt cooked up the Square Deal. We'll promise to savage K Street, execute far-reaching campaign finance reform, and, above all, right finance wrongs far and wide.

There's also one final policy, albeit one that I don't expect to be an integral part of any variation on the Big Idea, but something I think we can expect Obama to address. It's about the biggest problem facing the underclass in America today. What's the politically correct, safe answer? Lack of computers? Obesity and lack of access to nutritious food? Heart disease? They're all problems. But every rational person knows what is the biggest problem facing the underclass today, and it's fourteen-year-olds having children.

Until we own up to the problem of adolescent pregnancy as a nation and have a massive education program—that's right, you abstinence-only nuts, an education program, with science—to confront and deal with the issue head-on, every computer and every food pyramid and every S-CHIP program in the world is not going to solve teen pregnancy.

Please raise your hand if you remember the news coverage of

the seventeen girls who got pregnant at Gloucester, Massachusetts, high school in June 2008. It was everywhere. You couldn't
walk a step without seeing a magazine cover or hearing something
on the radio or television. That didn't need to happen. Sex education could have gone a long way toward helping these girls have a
firmer grasp on sex, pregnancy, and families.

Now that we've established a touchstone in current events, let's
look at the bigger picture. From 2005 to 2006, the number of pregnancies among girls aged fifteen to seventeen rose by almost 6,000,
to 139,000.[2] That's a 4.5 percent increase. That's huge. And it's the
first time since 1991 that teen pregnancies have risen over the
course of a year. If you haven't figured it out yet, I'm happy to point
to what was going right from 1992 until 2000—that's Clinton, and
reasonable, scientific, informed sexual education programs—and
what failed programs and policies began in 2000 that would be
coming home to roost in 2006—that's abstinence-only education.

It's been a long time since I was a teenager, but I seem to recall
that teenagers are pretty interested in sex. And, probably no matter what you do, short of locking them up (and probably even if
you do lock them up), they're going to have sex. With supply-side
economics and neoconservatism a very close second and third, I'll
nominate the idea of abstinence-only education as the least rational
political position of the last ten years. Republicans have poured
$900 million into abstinence-only initiatives that make our kids no
less likely to have sex, and a lot less likely to be safe when they do
have sex. And just to give you an idea of how absurd these programs were, they also targeted sexually active young adults up to
age twenty-nine.[3]

Look at any one of the ideas outlined above individually or the total
collectively. There's nothing most good Democrats won't favor.
Depending on your particular brand of ideological underpinnings,
there's some you probably like better than others, but none you'd
protest. Taken individually, these ideas have also all been around
in some form or another for quite some time. Most of them came

up during the campaign. They just haven't been part of a Big Idea recently.

Critics of the twenty-first-century Democratic Party, yours truly included, have been pointed in their criticism of Democrats' inability to present the country with these positions wrapped up in a cohesive, coherent narrative. After all, it's been forty years since the Great Society, and all we've got is a litany of policy proposals. Call them the Big Seven, maybe. It's not a narrative, it's a football conference of Democratic ideas. On its face, this is nothing but another litany.

All right, so we've gone this far. We dissected the history of the Big Idea and know now that it's often (if not always) just a new way of presenting existing policy proposals. Then we explored the failure of the last two Big Ideas and discovered the time is ripe for a Democratic Big Idea. We even decided what the components of the Big Idea are. What we still lack is a narrative or framework or rallying cry for the party—the Big Idea. By now, you're saying, Mr. Carville, will you please get to the point? You're also probably thinking, this lunatic doesn't have any idea of what the idea or the narrative ought to be.

But I do have some notion of what the Democrats' narrative has to be. In fact, everyone in the universe of sane, un-nutty, thoughtful people knows what the Big Idea has to be. I addressed it in the last chapter.

It's time to go back to the basic instincts of most Americans. They love their country. They're patriotic. Bring that sense of citizenship and community back into politics. That's exactly what Roosevelt and Kennedy did in their Big Ideas, it's what Obama did during the election, and it's a message he must now refine as president—and de facto head of the Democratic Party. Begala and I offered up the name "progressive patriotism" in *Take It Back*. I'm pretty attached to the name, but I'm open to ideas. Maybe we can steal a little mojo from the Roosevelts, call this new thing the "Real Deal."

Teddy had the Square Deal. FDR had the New Deal. Truman

had the Fair Deal. Now, as a party, let's push a Real Deal. It's a set of policies that responds to the realities that we face in the United States today in the wake of an administration that dealt in half-truths, lies, and outright fiction.

What are the realities? A recession. The growing income gap. Serious environmental and national security threats that are not, by the way, unrelated. A collapsing Social Security system.

The premise of the Real Deal is that it is the duty of this country and its citizens to recognize our problems and to come together to solve them. It's taking "Yes we can" a step further to "Yes we will," and applying it to the challenges the country faces today. Obama's laid the foundation, and it's up to all of us to keep building. Whether the problem is inequality or run-amok foreign policy, social programs we cannot afford, rising sea levels, the financing of tyrannical governments, ongoing perpetration of a permanent underclass—you name it—it's an American problem, one that we as a nation can and must solve. Onc could say that Obama began signaling his intent to involve all Americans in the process of solving these problems with his early cabinet appointments, especially with the selection of a few Republicans and the inclusion of his former opponent, Hillary Rodham Clinton, as secretary of state.

The sense of patriotism and community we share is where every Democratic Big Idea has ever come from historically—just as every conservative Big Idea has come from the notion that it's every man for himself. That's the fundamental difference between Democrats and Republicans: "all hands on deck" versus "every man for himself."

We know what we have to do as a party. We're armed with a set of tried, true, empirically proven, Harvard-approved, University of Chicago–blessed policies. But how do we turn receptivity and enthusiasm into solid and sustainable support for these initiatives? It's one thing to be for saving the environment; it's another to give up your SUV.

The truth is, none of these Democratic ideas taken alone sounds particularly politically attractive—at least not compared to the conservative Big Ideas. After all, what could be more attractive than the idea that lowering taxes would help everyone? That the government would take less, and, in return, you'd get more?

There's perhaps nothing more appealing than the promise that you could send a limited number of troops to a strife-torn country for a short length of time and, in return, be greeted and welcomed as liberators, cover all costs with that country's oil revenues, and build a nation respected by all.

I can already hear the commentators gearing up to shoot down the Democrats.

Just imagine Bill O'Reilly's apoplexy. He'll spew about how the Democrats are downers who don't understand American exceptionalism and the uniqueness of our great nation. Of course, Bill O'Reilly is the one who doesn't understand what's going on in our country right now. O'Reilly's on every night to say how well the Iraq War is going and to tell us it's the right of every American to drive an SUV or pickup as big as he or she might like.

At least I can tell you that they're probably not going to trot out some right-wing economist to chatter about saving your Social Security from the Democrats by sending payments into an investment account. After years of explaining very patiently that these mealy-mouthed Democrats just don't understand that the global economy makes us immune to the cycles of the past, the Republicans are holding their hats (and eating serious losses on the stock market).

Republicans' spin is old, and their policies have failed. The shaky logic of the policies that got us into the current situation—an unprecedented financial crisis, record foreclosures, rising income inequality, growing debt, billions more dollars flowing into Iraq, and thousands of Americans dead—is wearing thin.

The Republican Party is so divorced from reality it may take years for them to recover. They are profoundly deluded. Just listen to onetime leader of the Republican presidential nominee pack Rudy Giuliani, who, by the way, is not a member of the community of same people. He actually said the way to fix the problems of the Alternative Minimum Tax is through more tax cuts to the wealthy.

Then Giuliani said, and get this, the problem with American foreign policy is that America is not feared enough, and that what we need to do is go slap some more people around. More military commitments worldwide. Bingo. When conservatives say things like this, it gets even easier to argue that the Democrats are going to be in office for a while. Everyone but Rudy Giuliani and his neocon cohort understands that the United States has to take a more pragmatic and realistic approach to foreign policy. (That's realistic not in the sense of realpolitik but of common sense, something the Bush administration seems to have been sorely lacking.)

Every American election since World War II has been about expanding possibilities. The Real Deal is premised on two very basic and, in my opinion, near-inarguable assumptions. The first is that the urgency of certain fundamental adjustments to policy at home and abroad is all too evident. These repairs are all reflected in some form or another in the tenets of the Real Deal.

Second, after all the years of Republican b.s., and that's exactly what supply-side economics and starting wars with no idea of entrance or exit is—sometimes you just have to call b.s. what it is— the restoration of Americans' faith in the federal government will be a long-term undertaking. Obama's campaign and first months in office have proven that he, as an individual and a politician, is more than capable of capturing widespread support. Now Obama and Democrats in Congress must work to rebuild Americans' trust in government as a force of good.

If you pause and think about it, a Real Deal is exactly what the American people are looking for in political leadership—and it's exactly what they voted for in 2008 when they elected a Democratic Congress and President Obama. Americans, and the world, in fact, have been burned by quick-fix campaign slogans and speech lines that become public policy. Now the Democrats, led by President Barack Obama, must enact solid, sensible policies and repair Americans' relationship with government—they're ready to strike the Real Deal.

Conclusion

In the Introduction, I talked about the Dowd memo being the flapping of the wings of the butterfly. As historians dissect the great Republican collapse, they'll have much more of a record to work with than I do, but I do think it began when Karl Rove and Bush embraced the Matthew Dowd memo. There were a number of moments that, when we look back, they'll be as obvious in the future as they are today: Katrina, WMDs, beyond disbelief energy policy—and, of course, Terri Schiavo.

The Terri Schiavo case was the one instant in which it was revealed just how caught up the modern Republican Party is with the right wing. (The selection of Sarah Palin as John McCain's running mate may qualify as another.) Republicans mounted a Sunday night legislative effort, and Bush got jerked around like a dimestore politician, intruding on family matters.[1] There's never been a case of more asinine science or a more pathetic use of medicine. The autopsy confirmed what every doctor said was the case, even as right-wing preachers had the Republicans making fools of themselves. Eventually the Schiavo case will be seen as part of the unraveling, as much so as anything else. What will be more interesting than tracing the decline of the Republican Party in modern politics (although I am certainly enjoying it) will be observing its recovery. I'll be the first person to acknowledge that the United States will always have a pro-business, center-right political party. In the future it will probably be the Republican Party, but it will not be the one we know right now, or the GOP of 2000, either.

It's going to be fascinating to see how the Republican Party re-emerges from its current disastrous state. I'll be curious to see how Republicans weather the effects of the Bush-Rove-Dowd legacy. The consequences of losing an entire generation of voters will be monumental. I've spoken to a great many Republican pollsters, consultants, and supporters. Most of them admit they are sickened by the data; others say heartbroken. The country realized what every political strategist of either party realizes: the 2008 election proved just how dramatically the political terrain of the United States is shifting. Will the Democrats win every election for the next forty years? Of course not. Again, of course not. Woodrow Wilson and Dwight Eisenhower were elected during the opposite party's dominance. Nonetheless, the days of Republican ascendancy in presidential politics have either ended or are in the process of ending, and a Democratic majority headed by President Obama has emerged.

Epilogue: Why I Moved to New Orleans

The basic reason I moved to New Orleans is simply this: I like it there. My family's from there, my wife and I fell in love in that city, we got married there, and if you're fortunate enough to be able to live in uptown New Orleans, you have what is in my opinion as high a standard of living as anywhere in the world. Basically I love great food, good music, LSU sports, and family. Where else can I go and get all of that within an hour and fifteen minutes of my front door?

But there is something that is driving me more than just the obvious appeal and pleasures of living in New Orleans. And that is that, at my age, sixty-five in October, I so much would prefer to be a part of something trying to make it, as opposed to being a part of something that already has it made. It's like my view of politics. I always try to identify with the folks who are trying to make it and not the folks who already have it made.

That's the classic difference between a Republican and a Democrat. Republicans exist to protect what people have, and Democrats exist to help people have the opportunity to acquire the things that they need. Civil rights, education, women's rights, opportunity, health care, you name it. The Republicans are a party that is designed to protect wealth. We should always strive to be a party that is designed to help people attain riches, of which money is only one part. We move for financial security but, more than that, family security, and security from fear and threat.

The other thing is that New Orleans is a monument to what

harm bad government can bring about, and, moreover, how good people can overcome bad government. When your national policy is tax cuts for wealthy people and not levees and flood protection for all people, the result is inevitable. When your policy is political appointees over competence, the result is inevitable. When your policy is to blame everyone else for your problems as opposed to accepting responsibility for your inaction and ineptitude, the result is inevitable. However, people have seen through this, and they are starting to make real progress all across South Louisiana.

If I can contribute anything, however small, to this effort, and to the state and the people I love, I'll be all the happier and all the better for it.

The Story of a Friend
Who Survived
Hurricane Katrina

as told to Rebecca Buckwalter-Poza,
July 2008

The following story is that of a friend who was in New Orleans during and immediately after Hurricane Katrina. He showed tremendous bravery and resolve, moving his family to Texas until they had the opportunity to move back to New Orleans. For anyone who has somehow missed the scope of the tragedy in Louisiana and throughout the Gulf Coast, I strongly encourage that you read his profoundly illuminating story. In fact, if it were in my power to do so, I'd say it should be required reading for all Americans.

I. Katrina

I didn't come out that well propertywise, but everything else turned out pretty well. A couple days before Katrina, as a family we were trying to decide whether to leave, whether to stay, or whether to go to the Dome. I'm a driver, and two days before the storm I actually went to work. The airport was closing, so I took several people who needed to get away out of New Orleans. The next day, the day before Katrina, my family decided to leave. We packed twenty family members into three vehicles.

In New Orleans there were no gas stations to get gas, so all of us thought maybe if we just get on the road and got going we could get gas after we got outside of the city. But then we ended up sitting on the interstate and started to have car problems with one of the cars. We had to pull over to put water in the car, that sort of thing. We did manage to get from 10 to 310 to 90. Once we crossed over 90, we sat in a traffic jam. Once we got to Boutte, which was nine hours later, the sheriffs were out, saying that if you really need to get gas there's no gas between here and Lafayette. They said, if you can make it to Lafayette continue, but if you can't, you'll have to come up with another plan because there's no gas. Between the three vehicles we were down to about a quarter tank of gas. So we knew that we weren't going to be able to make it to Lafayette.

The plan then was to go to my grandmother's complex. My grandmother lives in a complex for the elderly off Johnson and Esplanade. It's about five feet off the ground, so we knew we were going to be safe. We had canned goods, we had a portable television, and we had a portable radio, so we went to the house. There were twenty of us inside a one-bedroom apartment just waiting out the storm.

That morning it was 5:30 a.m. when Katrina actually arrived. My two boys and I went out on the porch and watched as Katrina hit. We saw the hurricane as the trees were toppling over, as there was debris in the street, and power lines falling. We stood on the porch and watched it until about 6:45 a.m., when we determined we had enough. We went inside. The house was really hot, so we had to bust open a window to get air to come into the rooms. It was still raining outside, and there was water pouring in and everything, but at least we started to breathe better.

When we looked out, there was about a foot and a half of water in the street. I thought that was basically normal for a hurricane. Anytime there was rain there would be a lot of water. Then we heard on the radio that the 17th Street Canal had breeched and none of the pumps were working. Where my grandmother lived on Johnson Street between Esplanade and St. Bernard was about a mile away from the London Avenue Canal. My sister Sheila lives about four blocks from the London Avenue Canal. Even though she was with us, she'd already gotten word from someone else that that area was flooded. We all decided just to stay put where we were.

II. Getting Help

As the days went by, as the second day, then the third day, then the fourth day passed, we were watching the water rise, going from the second step to the third step to the fourth step. By day five, the water had reached the top step of the apartment building.

We were walking in water, and we could see five feet of water outside. We could see helicopters. Myself and my two sons went up to the roof of the apartment, the third floor, as high as we could go, and we waved a white sheet while helicopters were passing by. We were waving the sheet at them, and they'd wave back at us. That's how close they were. But no one was actually trying to rescue anyone. They were just filming.

The building we were in was an elderly complex. I decided, I told my mother, I'm going to go outside and see if we can get some help. I went through the back door where my grandmother lived and there was basically no one back there. There was a slanted stairway and I knew where it led to, but I couldn't see it, so I took a chance and just walked, and I fell into the water. When I stood up, it was up to my chest. So I knew it was five feet of water.

As I walked out of the back gate, I got out to Miro Street to St. Bernard. I looked around, walked back to Esplanade, looked around, didn't see anybody. The only people there were residents in the city scrambling to try to get someone to help them. So I walked back down St. Bernard around to where St. Leo the Great

School is, around the race track, then I cut across to Grand Route St. John. Just as I was approaching the city park, I see two guys or four guys in two different boats. When they see me they say, "Oh, how're you doing, where are you going?" And I said, I'm looking to be rescued.

They asked me to show where we were on a map they had. So they gave me this map, and I looked at this map, and I looked at the street patterns. I won't forget this conversation.

They questioned me, asking me, "How many animals do you have? How many people do you have? What's the situation with you?"

I said, "Well, we have no animals, just people. We're inside a house, and we're just looking to be rescued. But this map that you have, I don't live anywhere on this map. The map only goes to Broad Street, but I live below Broad Street, so you have to keep going down Esplanade or Saint Bernard."

They said, "Well, I'm sorry, this is the area we're designated to rescue in. I'm sorry, we can't help you."

I asked, "You can't help me?"

They said, "We're sorry, sir, you have a problem."

So I said, "Well then, I'm sorry, too, because you've got a problem."

"Okay, well, what's our problem?"

"The problem is, that I'm going to drown someone and take this boat from you."

"Wait a minute. Look, we're not supposed to do this but look we'll take you back to the vicinity you came from."

III. Getting to Safety

As I rode back to my family in the boat with these men who didn't want to rescue anyone outside of their area, I talked with them and explained to them that my family was in an elderly complex with my grandmother. There was no electricity. The folks in there all had respirators and breathing machines. I asked them if they could at least help the elderly. All they would say was, "I'll tell you what we'll do, we'll take you back there."

So on the way back to the apartment complex, they wanted to know where we were. We were in the Seventh Ward. They wanted to know what the streets around us were. So I said, to the right is Esplanade, to the left is St. Bernard. When we got to the top, they were looking at the complex and they could see the people sitting out on the porches and fanning themselves. One of the two of them had a radio and he was in communication with this helicopter above us. He was talking on the radio to the guy in the helicopter, telling him it was an elderly complex, explaining the situation and the area.

After he got off the radio, the guy said, "The good news is, this area will be rescued." Then he said, "They'll be back in about ten days."

The men in the helicopter started throwing water and food into the courtyard, into the water, from the helicopter. People started scrambling to get down and get the food. They actually made it more chaotic by just throwing things down out of the helicopter. So I said, "Well, let me get my family. You have to help my family."

They said, "No, we only wanted to take you home. If folks know these two boats are back here, they're going to rush them."

I said, "Okay, let me go in through the back door."

So I go in through the back door, and I bring out my grand-mother, my mom, my sisters, and my kids, and we all piled into this boat. They took us to I-10 and they said that was as far as they could take us. We walked from the on-ramp of the bridge over to the Convention Center. As we were walking down I-10, we heard stories of what was happening at the Dome and that sort of thing.

We decided not to go to the Dome. It seemed like our best chance was to go to the Convention Center, so we did. When we got there, though, the state police were in the streets, trying to impose order. They were saying that the Dome, not the Conven-tion Center, was where victims should go. Still, they told us that there were buses coming the next day to pick people up and take them to Houston. We got a tag to guarantee our family would be on a bus to Houston.

IV. Leaving New Orleans

We had no food, no water, nothing with us. I decided to go to the office my company had five blocks away to see if I could get us some drinks or something. Once I get there, one of the managers was there, hollering and screaming at me for not leaving. The whole place was surrounded by police. We had a cinder-block wall, and someone had busted down the cinder-block wall and was stealing all the vehicles.

When I went in, the owner of the place told me to make sure to take a car, whatever car I could find—"go get it and get out of here." I took a vehicle and went to the Convention Center, and then I began driving my family to Texas. I drove one group to Houston and then drove back, then I drove the other group to Houston. Then I drove both groups to Dallas. That's how we got to Dallas.

V. Dallas

We stayed in Dallas for thirteen months. What I remember from first moving to Dallas was a particular interview on the radio in which someone said that people should be very careful of the New Orleans refugees who were there. They said that the New Orleans people were in a survival mode, and everyone should be very careful about how they handled and dealt with them. They added that in the coming months they'd find out who the sex offenders were and let the citizens of Dallas know.

I can't forget WPAB. On one of the biggest talk shows in Dallas, this guy talked about the New Orleans citizens like you would not believe. I think from that particular point on, we didn't really have a chance in Dallas. That isn't to say that there weren't a lot of good people there—there were. One of the good people I met, who was really helpful to us, was a young lady who belonged to Central Baptist Church in Crandall, Texas. The church decided to adopt a family, and they pulled out our name—and we thank them.

When we first moved to Dallas, Dallas Housing Authority put us in an apartment complex in South Dallas and gave us free rent for three months. But the area that they put us in was mainly a housing project. There was shooting, people were selling drugs, and there was prostitution in front of the housing complex. So I went to the Dallas Housing Authority, and told them that I understood I couldn't be picky about where I lived, but I did not live this way in New Orleans. I asked them if there was anything they could do for me to get us out of this situation. I explained that I had my mother, my grandmother, and my little kids living in this complex.

They said I could do one of two things: accept where I was and live there for a year, or go off on my own. I slept on it that night, and I thought about it, and I just had to get away. So I caught a train, the blue line that came into town to get mail. Since we had already filled out forms at the reunion arena, and they said the mail would be coming soon, I said that I would go down and check on it and fill out the P.O. Box form at the Post Office. I was doing errands to keep myself occupied while I worried about this housing problem.

Coming back I caught the wrong train, and I wound up on the other side of Dallas. When I realized I was on the wrong train, I got off and started to walk around to see what was in the vicinity. I walked right into an apartment complex. Figuring it couldn't hurt, I asked if they took New Orleans residents. They said that they did and asked for my FEMA number. They asked how many apartments I would need. I needed three and I needed them now.

They said that we could have three, but it wouldn't be until December. This was mid-October. So I said, fine. That was fine for me. And it fit perfectly because the kids went on a Christmas break in December, and I had then already filled out the paperwork. And at the beginning of the Christmas break, we packed up and we moved to North Dallas into these apartments. It truly was a blessing for us. Life changed for us then. Moving from one area that was drug-infested, with prostitution, to a very good environment where the quality of life and the schools were much better was what we needed as a family. And we got involved in everything to take our minds off missing New Orleans.

We went to Rangers and Mavericks games. We went to Six Flags and the water-park. We did it all as a family every weekend. Every time we had a chance to do something as a family, we took it.

My daughter went to one of the top high schools in Dallas, and my other kids went to a local elementary school, which is also a very good school. They actually worked with the kids, which was so different from before.

At my son's high school, the boys on the football team decided to beat up the girls from New Orleans. They put up the names of the girls they were going to beat up on a wall, and after they beat them up, they crossed the name out. And my daughter's name appeared on this list. So I went into the school and talked to the principal, the assistant principal.

"That's my daughter's name. I understand the boys here are beating up the young girls. Is there anything you're doing about it?"

The principal said he didn't like my attitude.

"Let me stop you there," I interrupted. But he had his own ideas.

"No, let me stop you," he demanded. "Until you understand that you New Orleans people can't win, things are going to be this way. And your kids can't come in here and threaten our kids."

So, basically, the Dallas kids felt threatened by the New Orleans kids being there. The New Orleans kids went into the school system and rallied around each other as a support system, but the Dallas kids didn't want to believe that. They thought they were there to take over their schools and so they were fighting our kids. My daughter was fifteen years old at that time.

I said, "Okay, here's my situation. Since you already have a mind-set of how I'm supposed to be, here's my plan—my daughter, when she walks on your grounds, you have to protect her. If something happens to my daughter on your school grounds, I'll protect her myself."

They called the police and told them I was a terrorist threat. So I had to go in front of a judge. I didn't mean any harm, but I didn't like the response I was getting. The judge said it was a normal reaction, "but here in Dallas, we train our kids from a young age to be a little bit different." I said I was sorry, and he let me go.

VI. Spring Break

The counselor from my daughter's high school was from New Orleans, and everybody loved her. By the end of the school year, my daughter was known as Miss New Orleans. They thought the way she talked and the New Orleans music we played was very strange, but Dallas was very interesting. The kids adjusted better. But I was still getting the questions about home.

When can we go home? Where are my friends?

So, when spring break came along in April, I rented a van, packed everyone in, took them to New Orleans, and showed them the house. It had five feet of water inside. And then I showed them my grandmother's complex. Someone had already broken in and taken all the valuables. I showed them their old schools.

I think bringing them back to New Orleans was helpful for their experience in Dallas. Showing them that the wind blew the back part of the house and the roof off. Taking them into the Ninth Ward, explaining that everyone from New Orleans is now living in different places. Showing them that we can't go home right now. It was all helpful.

Once we got back to Dallas, their grades were different. They all passed the TAX test at the end of the school year, which promoted them to the next grade. The counselors said, "This is going to sound crazy, but we didn't think they were going to make it when they first came here, but they did, they passed." What a relief. By this time, we had spent thirteen months in Dallas.

VII. *Moving Back*

My sister was a sheriff in New Orleans and had contacts who were working on apartments around New Orleans. The city was trying to get the sheriffs and police to come back first, but my sister said, "I'm okay, but you know my family is in Dallas, and they really need to come back." They gave us a number to call but said that three apartments wouldn't be ready until mid-September. And then we got a call, "You can move home anytime now."

We immediately packed up. We weren't going to wait for that next week. Two days later, the whole family was packed up. That Sunday when we went to church, I spoke and said, "I have some good news, we found a place back home." The pastor asked how we were going to get home. At the time, we didn't really know. I figured we'd rent trucks and vans. But then a member of the church who owned a trucking company said, "You're not going to do that, we're going to send an eighteen-wheeler to your house, and he's going to drive you."

"We can't afford that," I told him. He insisted on taking care of it.

The day we were moving, about fifteen members of the church brought all kinds of furniture from storage. They had refrigerators and even found new mattresses, still wrapped in plastic. The crew of them unloaded all three of the apartments and loaded our furniture and all the furniture they gave us into the truck and sent us back home. My sister, grandmother, and I drove home, since my grandmother doesn't fly. But Barbie Bonds, who works for Southwest Airlines, got Southwest to fly the rest of my family members back home.

VII. Missing the Food

It was good to be home. I had enjoyed Dallas but I missed New Orleans like I never thought I could. I never thought that I actually loved my city like I do. I cried often in Texas with my grandmother.

She said, "Please don't let me die in Texas. If I die in Texas, I'll blame you. Take me home. If I die in Texas, it's on you." We went through this often.

One of our saving graces in Texas is that we'd occasionally go out as a family to restaurants. For the first six or seven months we were there, they didn't have any New Orleans products—Tony Chachere's Creole Seasoning, hot sauces, that sort of thing. And so for the first six months, I came back three times.

My momma would say, "Here's a few hundred dollars, here's an ice chest. Go back, and I don't care where you find it, bring some pickled meat, and bring me some beans back. Bring me some shrimp, something I can put in my gumbo, and bring me some andouille sausage." We all missed the food.

So I came back to buy hoghead cheese, hot sausage, and pickled meat for the beans. White beans, red beans—we ate all of it. My family slow-cooked beans and put andouille sausage and pickled meat in it. We mostly used Blue Runner beans but sometimes another type of beans, always on Monday. We'd have seafood on Fridays. It was a tradition at my family on Sunday we would fry chicken, with eggplant, mirlitons, and shrimp, so I would go home and get that. Food was important.

In Texas, they'd take the crawfish, boil it in the water, then they'd sprinkle pepper on top. So I said, "No, you're not seasoning the crawfish, you're seasoning the shell." At a place called Aw Shucks on Greenville Avenue, I explained to them how to do it, step by step, and they did it.

And there was one place in South Dallas that advertised "New Orleans Style Po' Boys," and I went and I asked for a roast beef po' boy. I ordered it "sloppy." The woman behind the counter looked at me a little bit, went in the back, came back out, and said, "The guy who makes the sandwich wants to know what you mean by 'sloppy.' "

I was in awe. Anyone that's ever had a New Orleans po' boy knew what "sloppy" meant. They were capitalizing off the New Orleans residents but they didn't know anything about New Orleans. We just couldn't find regular-type New Orleans food, so I had to come back and get hoghead cheese, pickled meat, and red beans. I drove back and forth to Houston five times, and it takes nine hours each trip.

VIII. *FEMA Sent Me*

At some point after the storm, I went to the medical station and I told the lady I was a diabetic. She asked how long it was since I'd had medicine. It had been a while. She stuck my finger and my sugar was 700 and something; she told me I needed to go and take my paper and my FEMA number to Lancaster Hospital in Lancaster, Texas, a suburb of Dallas. She said, "Take this, they're going to see you."

When I got to the hospital, they took the paper, looked at me, and put an IV in my arm. They then asked me where I was living in New Orleans, and I gave them a New Orleans address. I was at the hospital with an IV in my arm for a few hours. They got my blood sugar levels a good bit lower, then wrote a prescription for me for insulin supplies, testing strips, and a testing machine. I was grateful, and I thought that was the last of it.

Then, many months later, once we returned to New Orleans, I started getting letters looking for $3,700 for the hospital visit. So I'm calling the hospital and saying, "FEMA sent me there." It didn't help. I would never have gone if I knew, because I didn't have $3,700.

Letters and bills kept coming until I talked to a friend from the

Baptist Church in Crandall, Texas. He called the hospital and got them to forgive the bill. The same friends from that church also called during holidays and sent presents to our kids.

When that friend from the church went to bat for me with the hospital that was only one example of the kindnesses that community showed us. Coming from New Orleans and going into this strange community, I couldn't believe these folks embraced us the way they did. It was a white church, and they just took us as one of their own. Coming from New Orleans where most of us only come together for Jazz Fest or Saints games, it was very different. These people provided us with anything we needed. Some people said that the people in Dallas weren't very friendly, but most of them were.

IX. Organizing

Somewhere along the way, a group of six or seven guys from New Orleans got together and formed a group in Dallas. We were listening to the *Mark Davis Show* on WPAB and hearing him say things like "all the New Orleans people should go home." Davis always had people on his show saying that they gave money for Katrina relief and wished they could take it back because they didn't know where it went. Those sort of things hurt. The group of New Orleans guys got together to try to see what we could do for the other New Orleans residents in Dallas. A woman named Katie Neason from ACORN said we should form a group and come up with a mission and by-laws to see what we could do. Our main purpose was to show New Orleans residents that there was someone to help them in Dallas. But we didn't have any money.

The ACORN organization in Dallas saw us and heard us. They said if we came under their wing, they'd help us get money to do whatever we needed to do. So we became the ACORN Katrina Survivors Association. Branches of our organization opened in Houston, Memphis, Birmingham, Atlanta, and all across the South.

They used the model from Dallas to help people with housing and health care resources.

A friend named Greg Williams who worked with ACORN in Dallas said he wanted to take me to this church, a Presbyterian church, where every month they have a resource meeting to pull resources together to help the citizens of New Orleans. I went to the meeting and was listening to them talk about what they could do. I got up and introduced myself to the crowd, told them who I was, told them about our mission, and told them we didn't have any money. I told them the things we wanted to do, and they helped.

The way that we draw New Orleanians together is with music and food. So our idea was to throw a block party with New Orleans music with the help of the radio station. We'd then get health care providers and schools and other organizations to distribute information to our residents. We got Orleans Parish sheriff Marlin Gusman and other high-profile political figures in the city of New Orleans to become involved. We signed up 1,500 people to vote in the mayor's election and got a bus company out of Dallas to bring us to Shreveport to vote.

X. New Orleans in Washington

At one of our Katrina Survivors Association events, a man out of the ACORN national office in Washington, D.C., exchanged numbers with me. He was basically asking what I thought about how things were progressing. I didn't know it at the time, but he was actually interviewing me. ACORN invited our group to come to Washington for a rally. They even asked Ms. Neason and me to speak. It was four hundred or five hundred people. Speaker of the House Nancy Pelosi, Representative Barney Frank, and Representative Sheila Jackson Lee were all in attendance.

And then they said, "We need to take you to Mr. [Henry] Paulson's office. He is the head of FEMA." I had only a minute, so they gave me a script. But I just went completely off the script. I asked why more wasn't done to allow displaced New Orleans residents to vote. Why was it that, even though other countries have elections with polling booths for their citizens, we, scattered across the country because of Katrina, couldn't vote in the mayor's election in New Orleans? They wanted us to go back to the city to vote.

He said to me, "But we don't know where everyone from New Orleans is."

I said, "Mr. Paulson, please. Everyone signed up for FEMA. You know where we are. We'd like mail, and we'd like to know what's going on."

Mr. Paulson continued on that it was because of the Privacy Act that they couldn't put polling places outside of the state. And that was our meeting.

In the end, the only thing I can say is that there weren't enough hard decisions made for the city. The blame was on all levels—federal government, local, and state levels. Basically, I think the U.S. government wasn't prepared for the magnitude of this storm, and they didn't know how to come and help. Once they took FEMA out of the cabinet, they'd lessened it, and it didn't have the strength to help cities like New Orleans.

Notes

PREFACE

1. Steve Hargreaves, "Big Oil's money problem," *CNNMoney.com*, December 2, 2008; http://money.cnn.com/2008/12/01/news/economy/oil_profits_outlook/?postversion=2008120206.
2. Alex Koppelman, "Carville: Dean's Leadership Rumsfeldian," The War Room, Salon, November 15, 2006.
3. http://query.nictusa.com/cgi-bin/dcdev/forms/C00430470/3438 58/, accessed 12/8/08.
4. http://query.nictusa.com/cgi-bin/dcdev/forms/C00431569/336 278/.
5. Ibid.

INTRODUCTION

1. John W. Dean, "A Question-and-Answer Session with Thomas B. Edsall, Author of *Building Red America*," *FindLaw*, March 9, 2007.
2. "Clinton's Final Days: The Pump Don't Work 'Cause the Vandals Took the Handles," *Hotline*, January 26, 2001; Bob Ewegen, "Mean-Spirited Exit by Democrats," *Denver Post*, January 29, 2001.
3. Deborah Orin, "Bush Won't Go After White House Vandals—But Staff Is Cataloging Damage," *New York Post*, January 26, 2001.
4. Ibid.
5. David Goldstein, "GSA Says There's No Truth to White House Vandal Scandal," *Seattle Times*, May 18, 2001; Jake Siewert, "Who Got Trashed?", *The Washington Post*, May 27, 2008; Kerry Lauerman and Alicia Montgomery, "The White House vandal scandal that wasn't: How the incoming Bush team nudge-nudged a credulous press corps into swallowing a trashy Clinton story," *Salon.com*, May 31, 2001.
6. Jimmy Orr, "No practical jokes for Obama says Bush White House," *Christian Science Monitor*, 1/15/09, http://features.csmonitor.com/politics/2009/01/15/no-practical-jokes-for-obama-says-bush-white-house/, accessed 2/3/09.

CHAPTER 1

1. Jennifer Agiesta, "Behind the Numbers: Trust in GOP Reaches Record Low," *The Washington Post*, December 18, 2008.
2. Iraq, BarackObama.com, www.barackobama.com/issues/iraq/index.php, accessed 12/5/08.
3. "Bush Meets with Disaster Relief Task Force in D.C.," Fox News, September 1, 2005.
4. Eric Lipton, "Billions Later, Plan to Remake the Coast Guard Fleet Stumbles," *New York Times*, December 8, 2006.
5. "Ships That Don't Dare Sail," *New York Times*, December 14, 2006.
6. David Savage, "It's Time to Finish Inquiry into Cisneros, Counsel Told," *Los Angeles Times*, April 11, 2003; http://articles.latimes.com/2003/apr/11/nation/na-cisneros11, accessed 2/1/08.
7. Joe Conason, "Reagan without sentimentality," *Salon*, June 8, 2004; http://archive.salon.com/opinion/conason/2004/06/08/reagan/index.html, accessed 2/1/08.
8. Lisa Myers and Jim Popkin, "FBI Probes Nevada Governor for Corruption," NBC News, May 11, 2007.
9. Michael Carey, "The Demise of a 'Senator for Life,'" *Seattle Times*, August 5, 2008; http://seattletimes.nwsource.com/html/opinion/2008091590_stevensop05.html, accessed 8/5/08.
10. Ben Pershing, "The Culture of Corruption," *The Washington Post*, July 3, 2008; http://blog.washingtonpost.com/capitol-briefing/2008/07/the_culture_of_corruption_cont.html, accessed 8/1/08.
11. See James Carville on the late CNN show *Crossfire* on July 1, 2003, repeating, "I just will never get over it. I just can't get over it," in debate with Ralph Nader, *Crossfire*, CNN, July 1, 2003. See also Carville's comments on March 9, 2004, when he said of Bush, "I think he's really the president, but I think he was put in there by Scalia and Rehnquist and that whole crowd of bandits they got up there at the Supreme Court," *Crossfire*, CNN, March 9, 2004.
12. Jeffrey Toobin, "Too Close to Call," p. 33.
13. Ibid.
14. Jonathan Chait, "How the Netroots Became the Most Important Mass Movement in U.S. Politics," TNR, May 7, 2007.
15. U.S. Commission on Civil Rights, "Voting Irregularities in Florida During the 2000 Presidential Election," at www.usccr.gov (June 8, 2001).
16. Damien Cave, "In Florida Mailboxes, Harsh Attacks on Obama," *New York Times*, October 20, 2008; http://thecaucus.blogs.nytimes.com/2008/10/20/in-florida-mailboxes-harsh-attacks-on-obama/, accessed 12/8/08.

17. Seth Colter Walls, "Florida GOP Mailer: Obama 'No Friend of Israel,'" *Huffington Post,* October 28, 2008; www.huffingtonpost .com/2008/10/28/florida-gop-mailer-obama_n_138628.html, accessed 12/8/08.

18. Dara Kam, "GOP Mailers List Incorrect Sites for Voting," *Palm Beach Post,* www.palmbeachpost.com/localnews/content/state/ epaper/2008/10/20/1020gopvoting.html, accessed 12/8/08.

19. Ibid.

20. David Barstow and Don Van Natta, Jr., "Examining the Vote; How Bush Took Florida: Mining the Overseas Absentee Vote," *New York Times,* July 15, 2001.

21. "Obama Renews Call for Gonzales to Be Replaced as Attorney General," Web site of U.S. Senator Barack Obama, http://obama .senate.gov/press/070329-obama_renews_ca/, accessed 12/8/08.

22. *Boston Globe,* April 8, 2007.

23. *The Washington Post,* May 24, 2007.

24. *Think Progress,* 5/23/07.

25. *Los Angeles Times,* June 24, 2008.

26. Ibid.

27. Ibid.

28. Ibid.

29. Ibid.

30. "The Progressive Majority: Why a Conservative America Is a Myth," Media Matters, http://mediamatters.org/progmaj/report, accessed 4/1/08.

31. Larry Bartels, "What's the Matter with What's the Matter with Kansas?," 9/05, www.princeton.edu/~bartels/kansas.pdf, accessed 1/03/08.

32. Morris Fiorina, "What Culture Wars?" 7/14/04, www.hoover.org/ publications/digest/3010006.html, accessed 1/2/08.

CHAPTER 2

1. David Paul Kuhn, "Mehlman, Rove Boost McCain Campaign," *Politico,* www.politico.com/news/stories/0308/8911.html, accessed 12/8/08.

2. Tod Lindberg, "Pathetic Republicans," *Weekly Standard,* November 30, 2006, www.weeklystandard.com/Content/Public/Articles/ 000/000/012/948vawcv.asp?pg=2.

3. Lydia Saad, "As Independents Shrink, Democrats Gain," Gallup, 7/2/08, www.gallup.com/poll/108619/Independents-Shrink -Democrats-Gain.aspx, accessed 7/2/08.

4. "McCain Defends '100 Years in Iraq' Statement," CNN, February 1, 2008, www.cnn.com/2008/POLITICS/02/14/mccain.king/; www .youtube.com/watch?v=VFknKVjuyNk, accessed 6/1/08.

5. "McCain on When Troops Can Come Home from Iraq: 'That's Not Too Important,'" Think Progress, Center for American Progress Action Fund, 6/11/08, http://thinkprogress.org/2008/06/11/mccain-iraq-important/, accessed 6/12/08.

6. "McCain Conflates Shiite Iran and Sunni Al Qaeda, Needs to Be Corrected by Lieberman," Think Progress, 3/18/08, http://thinkprogress.org/2008/03/18/mccain-iran-al-qaeda/, accessed 4/1/08.

7. McCain Speech to the Council on Foreign Relations, November 5, 2008.

8. "Cheney Five Years Ago: 'We Will, in Fact, Be Greeted as Liberators,'" Think Progress, http://thinkprogress.org/2008/03/14/cheney-mccain-liberators/, accessed 6/1/08.

9. "New McCain Rips Old McCain's Argument That Bush's Tax Cuts Benefit the Wealthy," Think Progress, 2/17/08, http://thinkprogress.org/2008/02/17/mccain-wealthy-taxes/, accessed 2/24/08.

10. Robert Gordon and James Kvaal, "Five Easy Pieces and Two Trillion Dollars," Center for American Progress Action Fund, 3/21/08, www.americanprogressaction.org/issues/2008/taxagenda.html, accessed 4/2/08.

11. James Kvaal, "$4 Billion Among Friends," The Wonk Room, 3/27/08, http://thinkprogress.org/wonkroom/2008/03/27/mccain-petroleum, accessed 4/1/08.

12. "REPORT: McCain Plan Doles Out $2 Billion in Tax Cuts for the Biggest Health Insurers," 4/9/08, http://thinkprogress.org/wonkroom/2008/04/09/mccain-tax-health-insurers/, accessed 4/12/08.

13. Martin Wolk, "Cost of Iraq War Could Surpass $1 Trillion," MSNBC, March 17, 2008, www.msnbc.msn.com/id/11880954/, accessed 4/1/08.

14. "McCain's Plan to Cut Earmarks Would Eliminate Aid to Israel," Think Progress, Center for American Progress Action Fund, 4/16/08, http://thinkprogress.org/2008/04/16/mccain-aid-israel/, accessed 4/18/08.

15. "McCain's Speech Location Funded by Earmarks," Think Progress, 4/3/08, http://thinkprogress.org/2008/04/03/mccains-speech-location-funded-by-earmarks/, accessed 5/1/08.

16. "McCain's Plan to Cut Earmarks Would Eliminate Aid to Israel."

17. Gordon and Kvaal, "Five Easy Pieces and Two Trillion Dollars."

18. Ibid.; www.americanprogressaction.org/issues/2008/tax_agenda.html, p. 8.

19. Michael Cooper and Kevin Sack, "Federal Money in Health Care Plan from McCain," New York Times, April 30, 2008, www.nytimes

.com/2008/04/30/us/politics/30mccain.html?_r=2&oref-slogin& oref-login, accessed 5/1/08.

20. Michael Shear, "McCain Offers Market-Based Health Care Plan," *The Washington Post*, April 30, 2008, www.washingtonpost.com/ wp-dyn/content/article/2008/04/29/AR2008042902706.html, accessed 5/3/08.

21. "Rep. Burgess Is Wrong: McCain's Health Care Plan Would Undermine Existing Coverage," The Wonk Room, Center for American Progress Action Fund, 6/11/08, http://thinkprogress.org/wonk room/2008/06/11/existing-coverage/, accessed 6/20/08.

22. "NEW STUDY: McCain's Health Care Plan Raises Taxes on Millions of Middle-Class Families," The Wonk Room, Center for American Progress Action Fund, 7/2/08, http://thinkprogress.org/ wonkroom/2008/07/02/health-care-employment1-/, accessed 7/2/08.

23. Cooper and Sack, "Federal Money in Health Care Plan from McCain."

24. "Rep. Burgess Is Wrong: McCain's Health Care Plan Would Undermine Existing Coverage."

25. "NEW STUDY: McCain's Health Care Plan Raises Taxes on Millions of Middle-Class Families."

26. Roger Hickey, "The McCain Health Plan: Millions Lose Coverage, Health Costs Worsen, and Insurance and Drug Industries Win," Campaign for America's Future, April 29, 2008.

27. "NEW STUDY: McCain's Health Care Plan Raises Taxes on Millions of Middle-Class Families."

28. Sam Stein, "McCain in 2005: I 'Totally' Support Bush on the 'Transcendent Issues,' " *Huffington Post*, June 12, 2008; www.huffington post.com/2008/06/12/mccain-2005-i-totally-sup_n_106733.html, accessed 6/15/08.

29. *Chicago Tribune*, August 11, 2004.

30. Fox News, "Fox and Friends," February 8, 2008.

31. Associated Press, March 5, 2008.

32. NBC/WSJ via *CQ*, May 1, 2008.

33. Jeffrey Jones, "Americans Worry McCain Would Be Too Similar to Bush," Gallup, 7/1/08, www.gallup.com/poll/108490/Americans -Worry-McCain-Would-Be-Too-Similar-Bush.aspx, accessed 7/1/08.

34. *Washington Post* ABC News Poll, 5/14/08, www.washingtonpost .com/wp-srv/politics/documents/postpoll_051208.html?sid=ST 2008051400066, accessed 6/1/08.

35. Alan Abramowitz, "The Incredible Shrinking Republican Base," Larry Sabato's Crystal Ball, Center for Politics, 5/1/08, www .centerforpolitics.org/crystalball/article.php?id=AIA2008050101, accessed 6/4/08.

36. *Salon*, September 17, 2007.
37. 2008 Exit Polls, CNN, www.cnn.com/ELECTION/2008/results/polls/#USP00p1, accessed 12/1/08; *Salon*, September 17, 2007.
38. Abramowitz, "The Incredible Shrinking Republican Base."
39. Ibid.
40. Ibid.
41. Curtis Gans, "African-Americans, Anger, Fear and Youth Propel Turnout to Highest Level Since 1960," Center for the Study of the American Electorate, December 17, 2008.
42. "How Hispanics Voted in the 2008 Election," Pew Research Center, November 5, 2008; http://pewresearch.org/pubs/1024/exit-poll-analysis-hispanics, accessed 12/10/08.
43. Gans, "African-Americans, Anger, Fear and Youth Propel Turnout to Highest Level Since 1960."
44. "Obama Wins Big Among Youth, Minority Voters," CNN.com, 11/4/08; www.cnn.com/2008/POLITICS/11/04/exit.polls/, accessed 12/8/08.
45. "Turnout by Education, Race and Gender and Other 2008 Youth Voting Statistics," Center for Information and Research on Civic Learning and Engagement, Tufts University; www.civicyouth.org/, accessed 12/1/08.
46. CIRCLE Staff, "Young Voters in the 2008 Presidential Election," Center for Information and Research on Civic Learning and Engagement, Tufts University; www.civicyouth.org/, accessed 12/1/08.
47. "Background on the Millennial Generation," February 2007, Young Voter Strategies, www.youngvoterstrategies.org.
48. "Obama Wins Big Among Youth, Minority Voters," CNN.com.
49. *Los Angeles Times*/Bloomberg, June 25, 2008.
50. CNN Exit Polls, accessed 7/22/08.
51. Laurie Goodstein, "Obama Made Gains Among Younger Evangelical Voters, Data Show," *New York Times*, November 7, 2008.
52. Associated Press-Yahoo, July 17, 2008.
53. CNN Exit Polls, accessed 7/22/08.
54. Gallup, July 2, 2008.
55. Lauren Auerbach, "O'Reilly said question of whether humans are causing global warming is 'all guesswork,' " Media Matters, mediamatters.org/items/200803040011, March 4, 2008.
56. O'Reilly: "[I]rresponsible and lazy . . . that's what poverty is," Media Matters, 6/16/04.
57. Seth Ackerman and Peter Hart, "Bill O'Reilly's Sheer O'Reillyness: 'Don't Call Him Conservative—But He Is,' " Fairness and Accuracy in Reporting (FAIR), July/August 2001.

58. Ibid.
59. "O'Reilly: 'I don't see any difference between Huffington and the Nazis,' KKK," Media Matters, February 28, 2008; Steve Young, "Bill O'Reilly: 'No Difference Between (Arianna) Huffington, Nazis and Ku Klux Klan.' " *Huffington Post,* February 27, 2008.
60. "O'Reilly: FBI should arrest the 'clowns,' " Media Matters, Media Matters, June 22, 2005.
61. David Barstow, "Behind TV Analysts, Pentagon's Hidden Hand," *New York Times,* April 20, 2008.
62. "Iraq Dominates PEJ'S First Quarterly NCI Report," Project for Excellence in Journalism, 5/25/08, journalism.org/node/5719, accessed 6/1/07.
63. David Bauder, "Fox Gives Iraq War Less Attention" Associated Press, June 11, 2007.
64. "Online Focus: Brit Hume," 2002.
65. John Harris and Jim VanderHei, "Why McCain Is Getting Hosed in the Press," *Politico,* October 28, 2008, www.politico.com/news/stories/1008/14982.html, accessed 12/1/08.
66. Michael Scherer, "McCain's 7 Steps to Beating Obama," *Time,* May 12, 2008.

CHAPTER 3

1. Eric Lipton, "Safety Agency Faces Scrutiny Amid Changes," *New York Times,* September 9, 2007.
2. "Audit: U.S. lost track of $9 billion in Iraq funds," CNN, January 3, 2005.
3. Eoin O'Carroll, "How hot was 2008?" *Christian Science Monitor,* 12/30/08, http://features.csmonitor.com/environment/2008/12/30/how-hot-was-2008/, accessed 2/3/09.
4. Bryan Walsh, "The Planet Gets Cooler in '08. Say What?" *Time,* 12/16/08, www.time.com/time/health/article/0,8599,1866862,00.html, accessed 2/3/09.

CHAPTER 4

1. "Ex-Bush Aides Say He Never Recovered from Katrina," Associated Press, December 30, 2008.
2. Rick Jervis, "New Orleans' Population May Have Hit Plateau," *USA Today*, August 4, 2008.
3. "Bush designates Allbaugh FEMA director, Rove as senior White House adviser," CNN.com, 1/4/2001, http://archives.cnn.com/2001/ALLPOLITICS/stories/01/04/bush.announce/, accessed 8/4/08.

4. David Stout, "Agency Chief Facing Test of a Lifetime on Response," *New York Times*, September 14, 2001.

5. John Elliston, "A Disaster Waiting to Happen," *Indy Week*, September 22, 2004.

6. "6th District Returns English to Congress," *Daily Oklahoman*, November 9, 1988.

7. Florence Shinkle, "Mike Brown's Inquiry into Loathsome Horseplay Preceded His Rise to Emergency Czar," *St. Louis Post-Dispatch,* March 23, 2000.

8. Elliston, "A Disaster Waiting to Happen."

9. Ibid.

10. Will Bunch, "Did New Orleans Catastrophe Have to Happen? 'Times-Picayune' Had Repeatedly Raised Federal Spending Issues," *New Orleans Times-Picayune*, August 31, 2005.

11. Dean Roberts, "New Orleans District of the U.S. Army Corps of Engineers Faces $71.2M in Federal Cuts," *New Orleans City Business*, June 6, 2005.

12. Evan Thomas, "How Bush Blew It," *Newsweek*, September 19, 2005; "Press Gaggle with Scott McClellan," aboard Air Force One, en route to Andrews Air Force Base, MD, August 31, 2005.

13. "Katrina Timeline," courtesy of ThinkProgress.org, http://think progress.org/katrina-timeline/, accessed 6/1/08.

14. "Katrina was Category 3, not 4," CNN, December 21, 2005, www .cnn.com/2005WEATHER/12/21/katrina/index.html/, accessed 3/17/09.

15. "Files Show White House Knew Levees Had Failed on First Day," Associated Press, 2/10/2006 (as printed in the *L.A. Times*, p. A23).

16. NBC's "Today Show" via "Katrina Timeline," ThinkProgress.org, http://thinkprogress.org/katrina-timeline/, accessed 8/4/08.

17. Lara Jakes Jordan, "Levee breaches reported by 28 agencies as Katrina hit, documents show," Associated Press, 2/9/2006.

18. "Katrina: The Warnings Bush Received," Associated Press video, March 1, 2006, www.washingtonpost.com/wp-dyn/content// video/2006/03/01/VI2006030101864.html, accessed 8/4/08.

19. "Katrina: The Warnings Bush Received," Associated Press video.

20. "President Participates in Conversation on Medicare," WhiteHouse .gov 8/29/2005, www.whitehouse.gov/news/releases/2005/08/ 20050829-5.html, accessed 8/4/08.

21. Whitehouse.gov, www.whitehouse.gov/news/releases/2005/08/ images/20050829-5_p082905pm-0125-515h.html, accessed 8/4/08.

22. "FEMA director waited to seek Homeland help," Associated Press, September 7, 2005.

23. "President Participates in Conversation on Medicare," WhiteHouse

.gov, 8/29/2005, www.whitehouse.gov/news/releases/2005/08/
20050829-5.html, accessed 8/4/08.

24. Doug MacCash and James O.Byrne, "Catastrophic Storm Surge
Swamps 9th Ward, St. Bernard Lakeview Levee Breach Threatens
to Inundate City," *Times-Picayune,* August 30, 2005.

25. "President Discusses Medicare, New Prescription Drug Benefits,"
WhiteHouse.gov, 8/29/2005, www.whitehouse.gov/news/releases/
2005/08/20050829-11.html, accessed 8/4/08.

26. Editor and Publisher via "Katrina Timeline."

27. Evan Thomas, *Newsweek*, September 11, 2005.

28. Adam Nagourney and Anne Kornblut, "White House Enacts a Plan
to Ease Political Damage," *New York Times,* September 5, 2005.

29. Thomas, "How Bush Blew It."

30. "President Addresses Nation, Discusses Hurricane Katrina Relief
Efforts," WhiteHouse.gov, 9/3/05, accessed 8/4/08.

31. Manuel Roig-Franzia and Spencer Hsu, "Many Evacuated, but
Thousands Still Waiting," *The Washington Post*, September 4, 2005.

32. Bruce Nolan, "Mission Work Is Central to Ohio Congregation," Associated Press, 6/28/08,www.examiner.com/a-1463380~Mission_
work_is_central_to_Ohio_congregation.html, accessed 7/1/08.

CHAPTER 5

1. Jennifer Agiesta, "Behind the Numbers: Ideological Shift or Just
Complicated?", *The Washington Post*, November 13, 2008.

2. These Statistics drawn respectively from Associated Press,
5/30/08; *Boston Globe*, 4/12/08; Associated Press, 6/3/08; American University, 5/19/08; *538.com*, 5/28/08; Associated Press,
6/4/08; and CBS, 6/4/08.

3. Curtis Gans, "African-Americans, Anger, Fear and Youth Propel
Turnout to Highest Level Since 1960," Center for the Study of the
American Electorate, December 17, 2008.

4. Associated Press, June 3, 2008.

5. "Dan Morain and Janet Hook, Obama Has Cash Advantage," *Los
Angeles Times*, http://articles.latimes.com/2008/jun/05/nation/
na-money5, accessed 6/6/08.

6. Greg Sargent and Eric Kleefeld, "Multiple Oil Company Executives
Gave Huge Contributions to Electing McCain Just Days After Offshore Drilling Reversal," Talking Points Memo, 8/4/08, http://
tpmelectioncentral.talkingpointsmemo.com/2008/08/oil_company
_executives.php, accessed 8/1/08.

CHAPTER 6

1. FEC Filings by Hillary Clinton for President, http://query.nictusa
   .com/cgi-bin/dcdev/forms/C00431569/, accessed 6/27/08.

CHAPTER 7

1. McCain on His Computer Illiteracy: "I'm Learning to Get Online
   Myself, and I'll Have That Down Fairly Soon," ThinkProgress.org,
   July 12, 2008.
2. Carla Marinucci, "McCain Defends His Tech Smarts in S.F.: He
   says he's using computer more each day," *San Francisco Chronicle*,
   July 29, 2008.
3. David All, "Joe Trippi says . . ." www.davidallgroup.com April 5,
   2007. Accessed 8/4/2008 via WaybackMachine: http://web
   .archive.org/web/20070622195120; www.davidallgroup.com/2007/
   04/05/joe-trippi-says-republicans/.
4. Jose Antonio Vargas, "Online, GOP Is Playing Catch-Up," *Washington Post*, May 21, 2007.
5. "McCain Cashes In with Internet Fund-Raising Chat," CNN.com,
   February 11, 2000.
6. Ibid.
7. Gary Wolf, "How the Internet Invented Howard Dean," *Wired*, January 2004.
8. Ibid.
9. Michael Wolff, "Candidate.com," *New York Magazine*, September
   8, 2003.
10. Glen Justice, "Kerry Kept Money Coming with the Internet as His
    ATM," *The Washington Post*, November 6, 2004.
11. Justice, "Kerry Kept Money Coming with the Internet as His
    ATM."
12. Vargas, "Online, GOP Is Playing Catch-Up."
13. Andrew Rasiej and Micah L. Sifry, "Don't Believe the Online Fundraising Hype," *Politico*, April 18, 2007.
14. Ibid.
15. Ben Smith, "A Glimpse at the Obama Web," *Politico*—Ben Smith's
    Blog, www.politico.com/blogs/bensmith/0608/A_glimpse_at_the
    ;Obama;web.html, accessed 8/4/08.
16. ActBlue "Support," http://actblue.com/support, accessed 6/20/08.
17. www.february7.org/why.php.
18. www.blogads.com, accessed 8/4/08.
19. "Reid presses to keep administration honest on Iran," http://demo
    crats.senate.gov/newsroom/record.cfm?id=256815&, accessed
    8/4/08.

CHAPTER 8

1. Press release from Office of Senator Inhofe, July 28, 2003.
2. Chris Mooney, *The Republican War on Science* (New York: Basic Books, 2005).
3. Bill Blakemore, "Arctic's First Ice Free Summer Possible," ABC News 6/27/08, http://abcnews.go.com/Technology/story?id=5265092&page=1), accessed 6/29/08.
4. John Church and Neil White, "A 20th century acceleration in global sea-level rise," *Geophysical Research Letters*, 33: L01602, L01602, doi:10.1029/2005GL024826, January 6, 2006.
5. Intergovernmental Panel on Climate Change, *2.2.5.4 Mountain glaciers. Climate Change 2001 (Working Group I: The Scientific Basis)*.
6. Intergovernmental Panel on Climate Change, 2.7 Has Climate Variability, or Have Climate Extremes, Changed?, www.grida.no/climate/ipcc_tar/wg1/088/htm.
7. www.ipcc.ch/pdf/assessment-report/ar4/wg2/ar4-wg2-spm.pdf.
8. Greg Miller, "Climate Change Likely to Trigger Global Destabilization, Report Says," *Los Angeles Times*, www.latimes.com/news/nationworld/washingtondc/la-na-intel26-2008jun26.0.5875448.story, accessed 6/1/08.
9. http://inhofe.senate.gov/pressreleases/climateupdate.htm, and press release from Office of Sen. Inhofe.
10. Nicholas Thompson, "Science Friction," *Washington Monthly* (August 2003), www.washingtonmonthly.com/features/2003/0307.thompson.html, accessed 4/5/08.
11. Felicity Barriner, "White House Refused to Open Pollutants Email," *New York Times*, June 25, 2008.
12. J. R. Pegg, "US Senate Abandons Global Warming Bill," Environment News Service, June 6, 2008.
13. Casey Luskin, "Human Origins and Intelligent Design," Progress in Complexity, Information, and Design, Volume 4.1 (July 2005).
14. "The Theory of Intelligent Design: A briefing packet for educators to help them understand the debate between Darwinian evolution and intelligent design," Discovery Institute, www.discovery.org/scripts/viewDB/filesDB-download.php?command=download&id=1453, accessed 5/25/08.
15. "Evolution FAQ," PBS, 2001, www.pbs.org/wgbh/evolution/library/faq/cat01.html#Q02, accessed 5/1/08.
16. Raju Chebium, "75 Years after the Scopes Trial Pitted Science Against Religion, the Debate Goes On," CNN, July 13, 2000.

17. Gallup Poll, June 20, 2008.

18. Jeannette Catsoulis, "Resentment Over Darwin Evolves into a Documentary," *New York Times,* April 18, 2008.

19. Peter Baker and Peter Slevin, "Bush Remarks on 'Intelligent Design' Theory Fuel Debate," *The Washington Post*, August 3, 2005.

20. Mike Huckabee, "Debate Real-Time Response: Huckabee on Evolution," www.youtube.com/watch?v=1JC2ptcJxD4&feature=related; transcript, CNN, 6/5/07, http://transcripts.cnn.com/TRANS CRIPTS/0706/05/se.01.html, accessed 5/10/08.

21. Transcript, CNN, 6/5/07, http://transcripts.cnn.com/TRANS CRIPTS/0706/05/se.01.html, accessed 5/10/08.

22. "Ron Paul on Teaching Evolution," *Physics Today*, 1/10/08, http:// blogs.physicstoday.org/politics08/2008/01/ron_paul_on_teaching _evolution.html, accessed 5/10/08; video here http://youtube .com/watch?v=6JyvkjSKMLw.

23. Sam Brownback, "What I Think about Evolution," *New York Times*, May 31, 2007.

24. Stephen Pizzo, "Tom DeLay in His Own Words," Alternet, May 16, 2002.

25. Bruce Tomaso, "Obama: Let's teach science in science class," *Dallas Morning News*, 4/14/08, http://religionblog.dallasnews.com/ archives/2008/04/obama-lets-teach-science-in-sc.html, accessed 5/14/08.

26. Patrick Healy and Cornelia Dean, "Clinton Says She Would Shield Science from Politics," 10/5/07, www.nytimes.com/2007/10/05/ us/politics/05clinton.htm, accessed 5/1/08.

27. Mike Allen and Brian Faler, "Quotables," *The Washington Post*, 8/15/05,www.washingtonpost.com/wp-dyn/content/article/2005/ 08/14/AR2005081401037.html.

28. Audrey T. Leath, "Holt, Scientific Societies Oppose Teaching Intelligent Design as Science," *American Institute of Physics*, 9/12/05, www.aip.org/fyi/2005/131/html, accessed 4/2/08.

29. Ronald Bailey, "Evolutionary Politics," 1/8/08, www.reason.com/ news/show/124271.html.

30. Wayne Reynolds, "6,000 Year Old Earth," Independence Baptist Church, www.independencebaptist.org/Books_by_the_Pastor/The %206,000%20Year%20Old%20Earth.pdf, accessed 6/1/08.

31. Mission to America, "6,000 years," www.missiontoamerica.org/ genesis/six-thousand-years.html.

32. Jodi Wilgoren, "Seeing Creation and Evolution in Grand Canyon," *New York Times*, October 6, 2005.

33. *Real Time with Bill Maher*, 8/24/07, www.billmaher.com/?page_ id=200.

34. Wilgoren, "Seeing Creation and Evolution in Grand Canyon."
35. Chris Mooney, "Not a Geologist," *The American Prospect*, January 24, 2005.
36. "Is the Grand Canyon Proof of Noah's Flood?" Creation Science Evangelism, 5/29/08, www.drdino.com/readNews.php?id=49.
37. John Noble Wilford, "Grand Canyon Still Grand But Older," *New York Times*, March 27, 2005.
38. Leon Jeoff, "Faith-Based Parks," *Time*, November 17, 2004.
39. "About Us," Dinosaur Adventure Land, www.dinosauradventure land.com/aboutDAL.php, accessed 6/1/08.
40. Jeoff, "Faith-Based Parks."
41. Religion on Display in National Parks Christian Fundamentalist Influence on Park Service Decisions "Faith-Based Parks" Decried, PEER press release, December 22, 2003.
42. Elders in "Renewed concern about creationism at Grand Canyon National Park," National Center for Science Education, January 4, 2007, www.ncseweb.org/resources/news/2007/US/699_renewed _concern_about_creation_1_4_2007.asp.
43. "How Old Is the Grand Canyon? Park Service Won't Say," PEER press release, December 28, 2006.
44. Cornelia Dean, "Creationism and Science Clash at Grand Canyon Bookstores," *New York Times*, October 26, 2004.
45. "How Old Is the Grand Canyon? Park Service Won't Say."
46. Ceci Connolly, "Some Abstinence Programs Mislead Teens, Report Says," *The Washington Post*, December 2, 2004, www.washing tonpost.com/ac2/wp-dyn/A26623-2004Dec1?language=printer, accessed 10/20/07.
47. "Abstinence-Only Sex Education," PBS, 2/5/05.
48. Laura Sessions Stepp, "Study Casts Doubt on Abstinence Only," *The Washington Post*, April 14, 2007.
49. Jodie Levin-Epstein, "Fact Sheet: 'Abstinence Unless Married' Education," Center for Law and Social Policy, November 1998.
50. Rob Stein, "Premarital Abstinence Pledges Ineffective, Study Finds," *The Washington Post*, December 29, 2008.
51. "The Content of Federally Funded Abstinence-Only Education Programs," U.S. House of Representatives Committee on Government Reform—Minority Staff Special Investigations Division, December 2004, www.democrats.reform.house.gov, accessed 12/04/07.
52. Peggy Peck, "AMA: No Evidence That Abstinence Sex-Ed Works," FOX News, February 24, 2005.
53. Bearman and Brueckner, 2001; Walters, 2005.
54. John S. Santelli, et al., "Explaining Recent Declines in Adolescent Pregnancy in the United States: The contribution of abstinence and

improved contraceptive use," *American Journal of Public Health*, 91
(2007): 150, 153–54.

55. See R. A. Hatcher, et al., *Contraceptive Technology*, 18th rev. ed.
(New York: Ardent Media, 2004).

56. www.family.org/socialissues/A000000357.cfm.

57. www.cdc.gov/std/Hpv/STDFact-HPV-vaccine.htm#hpvvac2.

58. Ibid.

59. Katha Pollitt, "Subject to Debate," *The Nation*, May 12, 2005.

60. Thompson, "Science Friction," *Washington Monthly*.

61. *Meet the Press*, transcript for December 30, 2007, www.msnbc.msn
.com/id/22409176/page/3/.

62. *Scientific American Mind*, Feb/March 2006 and April/May 2006 issues, www.sciencentral.com/articles/view.php3?article_id=218392773
&cat=1_7, accessed 6/28/08.

63. Ellen Goodman, "A Vatican Retreat on Homosexuality," *The Washington Post*, www.washingtonpost.com/wp-dyn/content/article/
2005/12/02/AR2005120201511.html, accessed 6/28/08.

64. "Transcript: Bush, Kerry debate domestic policies," CNN,
10/14/04, www.cnn.com/2004/ALLPOLITICS/10/13/debate.tran
script/, accessed 6/27/08.

65. *Meet the Press*, transcript for December 30, 2007.

66. "Hotline's Todd oblivious to McCain's inconsistencies on gay and
lesbian rights," Media Matters, 1/5/07, mediamatters.org/items/
200701050005, accessed 1/27/08.

67. http://marriagelaw.cua.edu/Law/states/doma.cfm.

68. Kathleen Burge, "SJC: Gay marriage legal in Mass," *Boston Globe*,
November 18, 2003.

69. Dana Milbank, "For Foes of Same-Sex Marriage, It's the Thought
That Counts," 6/7/06, www.washingtonpost.com/wp-dyn/content/
article/2006/06/06/AR2006060601280.html, accessed 6/17/08.

70. "Excerpt from Santorum Interview," Associated Press, 4/23/03,
interview taped 4/7/03, www.usatoday.com/news/washington/
2003-04-23-santorum-excerpt_x.htm, accessed 6/1/08.

71. Ibid.

72. http://thomas.loc.gov./cgi-bin/bdquery/?&Db=d110&querybd=
@FIELD(FLD001+@4(Homosexuality).

73. Ibid.

74. Ibid.

75. U.S. Commission on Civil Rights, "Voting Irregularities in Florida
During the 2000 Presidential Election," at www.usccr.gov (June 8,
2001).

CHAPTER 10

1. James Carville, *We're Right, They're Wrong* (New York: Simon & Schuster, 1996), pp. 11–12.
2. Ibid.
3. "Presidential Economics Myths and Facts Laid out by Weiner and Larmett amidst 'Wild Stock Ride,' " *Business Wire*, August 16, 2007.
4. Michael Kinsley, "More GOP Than the GOP," *Los Angeles Times*, http://articles.latimes.com/2005/apr/03/opinion/oe-kinsley3, accessed 6/3/08.
5. Kevin Drum, "Democrats vs. Republicans on the Economy," *Washington Monthly*, 5/9/05, www.washingtonmonthly.com/archives/individual/2005_05/006282.php, accessed 6/1/08.
6. Larry Bartels, "Partisan Politics and U.S. Income Distribution," Princeton University, 2/04, www.princeton.edu/~bartels/income.pdf, accessed 5/2/08.
7. Larry Bartels, *Unequal Democracy* (Princeton: Princeton University Press, 2008), p. 31.
8. "Equal Time," MSNBC, December 21, 2000.
9. David Sanger, "OUTLOOK 1995; A Lingering Unease Despite Strong Growth," *New York Times*, 1/3/95, http://query.nytimes.com/gst/fullpage.html?res=990CE1DF1738F930A35752C0A963958260&sec=&spon-, accessed 6/15/08.
10. "Clinton: Pay Debt by 2015," CNN, 6/28/99, (http://money.cnn.com/1999/06/28/economy/clinton/, accessed 6/12/08.
11. Kelly Wallace, "President Clinton Announces Another Record Budget Surplus," CNN, 9/27/00, http://archives.cnn.com/2000/ALLPOLITICS/stories/09/27/clinton.surplus/, accessed 4/20/08.
12. Todd Wallack, "Recession Is Here, Economist Declares," *Boston Globe*, 3/15/08, www.boston.com/business/articles/2008/03/15/recession_is_here_economist_declares/, accessed 5/15/08.
13. *New York Times Blog*, April 9, 2008; *Courant*, April 10, 2008.
14. *Wall Street Journal*, March 13, 2008.
15. *The Street*, April 9, 2008.
16. Alan Greenspan, "We Will Never Have a Perfect Model of Risk," *Financial Times*, 3/16/08, http://us.ft.com/ftgateway/superpage.ft?news_id=fto031620081437534087, accessed 6/27/08.
17. "The Rich, the Poor and the Growing Gap Between Them," *The Economist*, June 17, 2006, p. 28.
18. Larry Bartels, *Unequal Democracy*, Princeton University Press, p. 20.
19. "The Way We Were: Comparing the Bush Economy with the Clin-

ton Economy," Joint Economic Committee, Democrats, Senator Charles E. Schumer, January 2007.

20. Nicholas Von Hoffman, "Inflation's Undertow," *The Nation* (Web only), August 8, 2007.

21. David Leonhardt, *New York Times*, July 18, 2007.

22. "Presidential Economics Myths and Facts Laid Out by Weiner and Larmett amidst 'Wild Stock Ride,'" *Business Wire,* August 16, 2007.

23. Bureau of Labor Statistics; Robert Atkinson and Julie Hutto, PPI's "Bush vs. Clinton: An Economic Performance Index" (October 2004).

24. "The Way We Were: Comparing the Bush Economy with the Clinton economy," Joint Economic Committee, Democrats, Senator Charles E. Schumer, January 2007.

25. Robert Atkinson and Julie Hutto, "Bush v. Clinton: An Economic Performance Index," October 2004.

26. "The Way We Were: Comparing the Bush Economy with the Clinton Economy."

27. Von Hoffman, "Inflation's Undertow."

28. "The Way We Were: Comparing the Bush Economy with the Clinton Economy."

29. Von Hoffman, "Inflation's Undertow."

30. Bartels, "Partisan Politics and U.S. Income Distribution."

31. Calculation of top 5 percent is based on the eleven states where population was large enough to conduct analysis—"Income Inequality."

32. U.S. Census Bureau, *Current Population Reports*, August 2006, www.census.gov/compendia/statab/tables/08s0689.pdf, accessed 6/26/08.

33. Von Hoffman, "Inflation's Undertow."

34. Hale "Bonddad" Stewart, "Worst Economy of Our Lifetime, pt. II," *Daily Kos*, November 5, 2007.

35. "The Way We Were: Comparing the Bush Economy with the Clinton Economy."

36. Bureau of Labor Statistics; Robert Atkinson and Julie Hutto, PPI's "Bush vs. Clinton: An Economic Performance Index," October 2004.

37. Ibid.

38. Frank Newport, "Consumer Confidence Remains Near Low Point for Year," Gallup, 12/23/08, www.gallup.com/poll/113560/Consumer-Confidence-Remains-Near-Low-Point-Year.aspx, accessed 12/23/08.

39. Eduardo Porter, "This Time, It's Not the Economy," *New York Times*, October 24, 2006.

40. Dick Morris, *The Hill*, June 27, 2007.
41. "Morris claimed 'Bush's ratings on the economy' and terrorism 'are not bad'—based on what?," Media Matters, June 27, 2007.
42. "George W. Bush's Overall Job Approval Drops," ARG, 6/20/08, http://americanresearchgroup.com/economy/, accessed 6/28/08.
43. Peter Nicholas, "If It Is the Economy, GOP May Be in Trouble," *Los Angeles Times*, November 9, 2007.
44. October 9 Republican Debate Transcript, MSNBC, www.msnbc .msn.com/id/21309530/.
45. Transcript of October 9 Republican Debate, MSNBC.
46. Nicholas, "If It Is the Economy, GOP May Be in Trouble."
47. Transcript of Republican Presidential Candidates Debate, MSNBC, 10/9/07, www.msnbc.msn.com/id/21221689/, accessed 6/10/08.
48. Nicholas, "If It Is the Economy, GOP May Be in Trouble."
49. Ibid.
50. Bureau of Labor Statistics, US Department of Labor, www.bls.gov/ webapps/legacy/cpsatab3.htm, accessed 6/27/08.
51. U.S. Census Bureau, Current Population Reports, August 2006, http://www.census.gov/compendia/statab/tables/08s0674.pdf, accessed 6/28/08.
52. Ibid.
53. Ibid.
54. Ibid.
55. "After Complaints, Econ Data Portal to Stay Open, Real Time Economics," *Wall Street Journal*, 2/21/08, http://blogs.wsj.com/ economics/2008/02/21/after-complaints-econ-data-portal-to-stay -open/, accessed 6/20/08.
56. "EconomicIndicators.gov," *Forbes*, http://63.240.4.179/bow/b2c/ review.jhtml?id=7136, accessed 6/27/08.
57. "Bush Administration Hides More Data, Shuts Down Website Tracking U.S. Economic Indicators," *Think Progress*, 2/13/08, http://thinkprogress.org/2008/02/13/economic-indicators/, accessed 6/20/08.
58. Sen. Chuck Schumer, press release, 2/20/08, http://jec.senate .gov/Releases/02.21.08%20Economic%20Indicators%20victory.pdf, accessed 6/1/08.
59. "After Complaints, Econ Data Portal to Stay Open," Real Time Economics Blog, *Wall Street Journal,* blogs.wsj.com/economics/2008/ 02/21/after-complaints-econ-data-portal-to-stay-open, accessed 6/12/08.
60. Steve Hargreaves, "Who's to Blame for $4 Gas?" *CNN Money*, 5/22/08, http://money.cnn.com/2008/05/20/news/economy/gas _price_history/index.htm, accessed 7/1/08.

61. Robert Samuelson, "Let's Shoot the Speculators," *Newsweek*, 7/14/08, http://www.newsweek.com/id/143786, accessed 7/1/08.

62. Richard Benedetto, "Cheney's Energy Plan Focuses on Production," *USA Today*, 5/1/01, www.usatoday.com/news/washington/2001-05-01-cheney-usat.htm, accessed 7/1/08.

63. Arianna Huffington, "Governor Davis and the Failure of Power," *Salon.com*, 1/27/01, http://archive.salon.com/politics/feature/2001/01/27/power/index.html, accessed 7/1/08.

64. Paul Krugman, "Delusions of Power," *New York Times*, March 28, 2006.

CHAPTER 11

1. Scott Keeter, Juliana Horowitz, Alec Tyson, "Young Voters in the 2008 Election," Pew Research Center, 11/12/08, http://pew research.org/pubs/1031/young-voters-in-the-2008-election, accessed 11/14/08.

2. Mark Hugo Lopez and Emily Kirby, "Electoral Engagement Among Minority Youth," CIRCLE, July 2005.

3. See D. O. Sears and S. Levy, "Childhood and Adult Political Development," in D. O. Sears, L. Huddy, and R. Jervis, eds., *Oxford Handbook of Political Psychology* (Oxford: Oxford University Press, 2003), pp. 60–109.

4. Angus Campbell, Phillip Converse, Warren Miller, and Donald Stokes. *The American Voter.* Chicago: University of Chicago Press, 1960.

5. Sears and Levy, "Childhood and Adult Political Development."

6. D. Green and B. Palmquist, *Political Behavior*, vol. 16, no. 4 (December 1994): 437–46.

7. Jennifer Agiesta, "Behind the Numbers: Ideological Shift or Just Complicated?," *The Washington Post*, November 13, 2008.

8. Gans, "African-Americans, Anger, Fear and Youth Propel Turnout to Highest Level Since 1960."

9. National Youth Survey, Democracy Corps, March 2009.

10. Norman Ornstein, "The Curse of the Six-Year Itch," *Atlantic Monthly* (March 1986), www.theatlantic.com/politics/polibig/ornstein.htm, accessed 5/1/08.

11. National Youth Survey, Democracy Corps, March 2009.

12. CBS Poll: "Economy Worries Young Voters," CBS News, 4/21/08, www.cbsnews.com/stories/2008/04/21/opinion/polls/main4029859.shtml?source=RSSattr=HOME_4029859, accessed 5/1/08.

13. Jeannine Aversa, "Jobless Rate Climbs as 51,000 Jobs Vanish," Associated Press, August 1, 2008.

14. CBS Poll: "Economy Worries Young Voters."

15. Nicholas Kristof, "Cheney's Virtue," *International Herald Tribune*, 8/20/07, www.iht.com/articles/2007/08/20/opinion/edkristof .php, accessed 1/1/08.
16. National Priorities Project, www.nationalpriorities.org/tradeoffs? location_type=1&state=888&program=577&tradeoff_item_item= 365&submit_tradeoffs=Get+Trade+Off, accessed 8/5/08.

CHAPTER 12

1. Pew Research Center, May 14, 2008.
2. Paul Begala and James Carville, *Take It Back* (New York: Simon & Schuster, 2006), p. xi.

CHAPTER 13

1. ABC News/Washington Post Poll, 6/16/2008.
2. Elizabeth Landau, "Report: Teen pregnancies up for the first time in 15 years," CNN, July 11, 2008.
3. L. Finer, *Trends in Premarital Sex in the United States, 1954–2003*, Public Health Reports, 2007; 23: 73.; U.S. Census Bureau, Special and "Unmarried and Single Americans Week, Sept. 17–23, 2006," press release, August 10, 2006, www.census.gov/Press-Release/ www/releases/archives/facts_for_features_special_editions/0072 85.html, accessed July 3, 2008.

CONCLUSION

1. Carl Hulse and David Kirkpatrick, "House Members Hold Sunday Night Session on Schiavo Bill," 3/20/05, www.nytimes.com/ 2005/03/20/politics/20cnd-debate.html?pagewanted=print&positi on=, accessed 7/20/08.

Acknowledgments

One of the great fictional Louisianians of all time, Blanche DuBois, said famously that she always depended on the kindness of strangers. This real Louisianian has always depended on the kindness of friends.

More friends than I can possibly name here contributed their time, energy, intelligence, and insight to this book. To try to recognize all of you would inevitably mean that I would slight one of you, and that is something I never want to do.

So I'll just say that y'all know who you are, and I know who you are, and I'm grateful for your help and blessed by your friendship.

About the Author

James Carville is the best-known and most-loved political consultant in American history. He is also a speaker, talk-show host, actor, and author with six *New York Times* bestsellers to his credit. Part of a large southern family, he grew up without a television and loved to listen to the stories his mama told. Mr. Carville lives with his wife, Mary Matalin, and their two daughters in New Orleans.